FUTURE OF JOBS IN FINANCE

Growth Insight Global Finance

What CFOs & Global Leaders Predict About the Future of Accounting & Finance Careers

SRIPAL JAIN (CA, CPA)

notionpress.com

INDIA • SINGAPORE • MALAYSIA

ISBN
Paperback 979-8-90451-655-0
Hardcase 979-8-90540-319-4

Contents

About the Leaders

JAYESH SANGHRAJKA

CFO, Infosys

Jayesh Sanghrajka represents the modern CFO as a steward of enterprise value. As CFO of Infosys, his perspective reflects how finance is moving beyond reporting and control into a more strategic role at the center of business decision-making. His views in this book highlight a future in which routine work is steadily automated, while finance leaders are expected to shape outcomes, guide capital, and help organizations navigate change with discipline and judgment.

RAGHURAM KRISHNAN

Senior Director & CFO, Adobe India

Raghuram Krishnan brings the perspective of a finance leader operating inside one of the world's most technology-driven environments. As Senior Director and CFO at Adobe India, he sees finance not as a back-end support function but as a driver of enterprise decisions and long-term value creation. His contribution to this book reflects the shift from finance as scorekeeping to finance as a source of insight, judgment, and strategic partnership.

NISHANT MOHTA

Head of Finance - India, Invesco

Nishant Mohta's journey reflects a finance career built with depth, discipline, and deliberate learning. Beginning with Company Secretaryship and Chartered Accountancy, and later adding a CPA during his time in the United States, he has built a broad finance leadership perspective grounded in both qualification and experience. In this book, he speaks to the enduring importance of trust, technical credibility, and the evolution of finance toward becoming a stronger business advisory function.

TEJASWINI RAJWADE

CFO, Technology Sector

Tejaswini Rajwade brings more than three decades of finance leadership experience across multiple roles and geographies. Her career reflects a steady build across financial, operational, and strategic responsibilities, leading to the CFO role through breadth rather than narrow specialization. Her perspective in this book is especially valuable for its clarity: AI may transform large parts of finance, but curiosity, courage, adaptability, and human judgment will remain the qualities that distinguish future leaders.

SHRENIK SHAH

Managing Director, Armanino India LLP

Shrenik Shah has built his career at the intersection of accounting, advisory, people leadership, and operational scale. From foundations in tax compliance and client servicing, he moved into leadership roles focused on building teams, driving efficiency, and expanding the India practice of a global professional services firm. His chapter in this book captures the future of accounting as a shift from transaction processing to insight, analytics, AI-enabled workflows, and business partnership.

SHAILESH HARIBHAKTI

Chairman, Shailesh Haribhakti Associates

Shailesh Haribhakti brings one of the broadest and most unconventional career arcs in this book. He describes himself as living his fifth professional life: student, teacher at IIMA, chairman of a major accounting firm, sustainability professional, and now AI-led consultant. His perspective is both expansive and grounded, emphasizing that while routine work will disappear, research, discovery, human sensitivity, ethics, and the orchestration of value will remain central in an AI-driven future.

BALAJI RANGANATHAN

Senior Audit Director, Wells Fargo

Balaji Ranganathan's career spans nearly two decades in external audit and fifteen years in internal audit, giving him a rare vantage point across the assurance profession. His experience reflects the shift from traditional periodic audits toward more embedded, continuous, and risk sensitive forms of oversight. In this book, he offers a clear view of how AI will reshape internal audit: automating repetitive mechanics while increasing the importance of judgment, skepticism, ethics, and interpretation.

ANKIT GHEEDIA

Group Manager, Microsoft

Ankit Gheedia brings a technology sector perspective shaped by organizational change, continuous learning, and the rapid rise of AI. He sees the next decade not as a period of marginal improvement, but of complete reimagination in how work is structured and executed. His contribution to this book stands out for its urgency: in a world where a large share of current activities may be automated, the most valuable professionals will be those who think critically, ask the right questions, adapt quickly, and keep experimenting.

VISH DHINGRA

Partner, Big 4 firms

With more than three decades in professional services across firms including KPMG, EXL, and Big 4 firms, Vish Dhingra brings deep experience in business consulting, risk consulting, and finance process improvement. He has worked globally across sectors and cultures and is known for building new propositions, driving business growth, and developing future leaders. In this book, he offers one of the strongest formulations of finance's future: autonomous accounting will reshape controllership, and the professionals who thrive will be techno-functional finance engineers.

VIVEK C

Head of Finance, Technology Sector

Vivek C's journey spans Big Four audit, regional APAC finance leadership, controllership, and transformation roles in the technology sector. Having worked across both traditional and digital operating models, he brings a practical view of AI's role in everyday finance execution. His contribution to this book emphasizes that future finance teams will look materially different: recurring work will be automated, AI adoption will become a core performance lever, and finance leaders will increasingly be judged by how effectively they build AI-ready teams.

ABHISHEK GUPTA

CFO, Livspace

Abhishek Gupta's finance career has been shaped by a series of deliberate transitions across some of India's most significant consumer and technology businesses, including ITC, Hindustan Unilever, Flipkart, Myntra, and Livspace. His leadership journey spans audit, commercial finance, global controls, sales finance, supply chain finance, category finance, and large-scale transformation. In this book, he brings one of the most comprehensive views of finance's future: AI will absorb tasks, but judgment, leadership, ethics, investor confidence, and value creation will remain firmly human.

Preface

There was a time when finance could be explained in a few familiar words.

Precision.

Discipline.

Trust.

The numbers had to be right.

The controls had to hold.

The reports had to be accurate.

For decades, that was the core of the profession.

And in many ways, it still is.

But now something deeper is changing.

Artificial Intelligence is no longer sitting outside finance as one more tool to be tested, adopted, or postponed. It is moving into the heart of the function itself. What once required teams, time, and repetition can now be done faster, smarter, and often more accurately by machines.

Accounting is changing.

Audit is changing.

Reporting is changing.

Risk is changing.

And, with all of that, the meaning of a finance career is changing too.

This book emerges from conversations with leaders who are not watching that shift from a distance. They are living it from inside the profession.

They are building teams through it, making decisions through it, and in many cases, shaping what finance itself is becoming.

And across these conversations, one message appears again and again.

Routine finance work will shrink.

Judgment, interpretation, and decision-making will rise.

AI fluency will become a basic professional expectation.

And careers will no longer be linear in the old way. They will be adaptive, layered, and constantly evolving.

This book is written for the people standing at the edge of that future.

For students trying to understand whether finance is still the right path.

For young professionals wondering what skills will keep them relevant.

For career switchers looking at finance not as it was, but as it is becoming.

At the same time, this book also reflects a belief that lies at the heart of Simandhar Education: that success in finance will no longer come from qualification alone. Qualifications still matter. Fundamentals still matter. But the future will belong to those who combine conceptual depth with technological awareness, business judgment, and an adaptive mindset.

This is not a textbook.

It is not a prediction report written from a distance.

It is a practitioner-led view of a profession in transition.

If you read this book carefully, you will not only understand what is changing.

You will begin to understand what the future of finance will demand from you.

Introduction

There was a time when finance could be described in fairly predictable terms.

A good finance team was one that closed the books on time.

Prepared the reports accurately.

Explained the variance clearly.

Protected the controls.

And ensured nothing unpleasant emerged after the quarter had ended.

It was a function built on discipline, reliability, and rigor. A profession that rewarded accuracy, memory, method, and patience. If you were technically strong, careful with detail, and willing to put in the hours, finance offered a long and respectable career path.

That world is not disappearing.

But it is changing so fast that, in another decade, it may be hard to recognize the old shape of the profession inside the new one.

That is why I wrote this book.

When I began speaking to CFOs and senior leaders across technology, accounting, consulting, banking, asset management, retail, audit, and finance transformation, I expected to hear the usual range of opinions. Some optimism, some caution, a few fashionable claims about AI, and a few defensive arguments about why finance would "always remain the same."

What I heard instead was more serious and more interesting.

These leaders were not talking about AI as one more tool in the finance toolkit. They were talking about a structural change in the function itself.

Not just faster spreadsheets.

Not just smarter dashboards.

Not just automation of a few back-office tasks.

But a redefinition of what finance teams do, how they create value, how they are staffed, what skills they require, what kinds of people will rise, and what kinds of roles will slowly lose relevance.

That is the central idea running through this book.

The future of jobs in finance is not a story about replacement alone.

It is a story about transition.

The value in finance is moving.

It is moving away from repetitive execution and toward judgment.

Away from data preparation and toward interpretation.

Away from static reporting and toward real-time decision support.

Away from routine processing and toward business partnership.

Away from functional insulation and toward enterprise influence.

That shift is already underway.

The leaders in this book may disagree on pace. Some believe the change will be gradual. Some believe entire functions will be unrecognizable in less than ten years. Some are deeply optimistic about AI's role. Others are more cautious, especially when it comes to regulation, ethics, and the real messiness of corporate data.

But on one issue, there is striking alignment.

If a task can be described as repetitive, rule-based, data-intensive, and predictable, AI will increasingly do it faster, cheaper, and often more accurately than humans.

That includes many of the jobs that traditionally formed the base of the finance pyramid:

- manual reconciliations
- transaction-heavy accounting
- routine AP and AR work

- standard reporting packs
- repetitive variance analysis
- document-heavy coordination
- sampling-based audit procedures
- low-end compliance preparation
- information aggregation roles that once consumed entire teams

This does not mean finance is becoming less important.

In fact, the opposite may be true.

As machines take over the lower-value layers of work, the finance profession is being forced upward. Finance leaders are being asked not merely to report the business, but to help think the business. To shape decisions. To govern AI outputs. To design better control systems. To allocate capital with more insight. To understand risk in new forms. To tell the story behind the numbers, not just prepare them.

This is why so many of the leaders I spoke with used language that would have sounded unusual in finance even ten years ago.

They spoke of the CFO as a "Value Officer."

As a "Chief Value Architect."

As a "Steward of enterprise value."

As a stronger co-pilot to the CEO.

As a governor of technology, data, and AI-led decision systems.

This is not cosmetic language.

It reflects a real expansion of responsibility.

The CFO of the future will still care about reporting, controls, treasury, tax, and compliance. But those will increasingly run through intelligent systems, automated workflows, and AI assisted layers of review. The true focus of the finance leader will move toward what remains irreducibly human:

- strategic judgment
- capital allocation
- stakeholder trust

- investor communication
- ethical reasoning
- crisis navigation
- organizational leadership
- building teams that can work in hybrid human-machine systems

That last point matters more than many people realize.

This is not only a book about AI.

It is also a book about careers.

And careers, unlike technology, are deeply personal.

Every student who is currently doing a B.Com, BBA, CA, CPA, CMA, CFA, MBA, or any finance-adjacent degree is really asking some version of the same question:

What kind of professional should I become so that I remain useful in the future?

The answers in this book are neither identical nor simplistic, but they converge around a few themes.

First, degrees still matter. They build the base. They help one enter the profession. They provide language, structure, discipline, and credibility. But the degree is no longer the differentiator it once was. It may get you shortlisted. It will not carry your whole career.

Second, continuous learning is no longer optional. Many of the leaders in this book are explicit about this. A one-time qualification is not enough in a world where tools, expectations, and operating models are changing rapidly. The real professional advantage now lies in learning agility.

Third, hybrid capability is becoming the new premium.

The future finance professional will need to combine:

- finance depth
- data literacy
- technology fluency
- AI awareness

- communication skill
- business context
- professional skepticism
- judgment

In older models, these capabilities could live in separate people. In future models, especially leaner and more AI-enabled ones, they will need to coexist more often in the same person.

Fourth, mindset matters more than many people think.

Some of the strongest leaders in this book did not speak first about certification or software. They spoke about curiosity, courage, adaptability, ownership, discipline, integrity, the ability to ask better questions, the ability to keep learning before one is forced to, and the willingness to challenge both old processes and new machine outputs.

That is a useful warning.

Because AI will not merely reward the technically strongest.

It will also expose the mentally rigid.

And finally, there is the question of what remains human.

This is where the book moves beyond career planning into something deeper.

Again and again, leaders returned to the same set of ideas.

AI can assist in analysis.

It cannot own accountability.

AI can process scale.

It cannot carry moral responsibility.

AI can generate outputs.

It cannot build trust.

AI can flag patterns.

It cannot fully understand context.

AI can accelerate work.

It cannot replace integrity, conviction, or the courage to speak truth in the room where it matters.

That, to me, is the most reassuring insight in all these conversations.

The future of finance is not less human.

It is more demanding of human quality at a higher level.

The mechanical layers may shrink.

The moral and judgment layers will become more exposed.

In the old world, one could build a decent finance career while remaining mostly invisible inside the process. In the new world, that will be harder. As routine work gets automated, the people who remain will be those whose thinking, communication, judgment, and credibility stand out.

This makes the profession more challenging.

It also makes it more meaningful.

Because finance, at its best, was never really about numbers alone.

It was about stewardship.

About helping businesses create and protect value.

About balancing ambition with discipline.

About seeing risk before it becomes damage.

About helping capital go where it is most useful.

About ensuring trust survives scale.

Those responsibilities do not disappear in the age of AI.

They intensify.

This book, then, is not a book of forecasts for their own sake. It is a book of working perspectives from people who are already shaping and living this transition. Some are CFOs, some are business leaders, some are audit, accounting, consulting, or transformation professionals. Some work in old-economy settings transformed by new tools. Some work at the heart of technology itself.

Together, they do not offer a single grand theory.

They offer something better.

A set of real, grounded, experience-backed ways to think about the future.

You will find optimism here, but not naïveté.

You will find ambition here, but also caution.

You will find respect for technology, but not surrender to it.

You will find a consistent insistence that the finance professional of the future must become larger than the tasks that are now being automated.

That is the real invitation of this book.

Not to fear AI.

Not to worship AI.

But to understand where the profession is going, and to prepare deliberately for it.

If you are a student, this book will help you think beyond the old degree-to-job formula and ask what capabilities will matter over the next twenty years.

If you are a young professional, it will help you see which parts of your current role are likely to be automated and where you must consciously migrate your value.

If you are already in finance leadership, it may help you ask harder questions about how your team should evolve, what talent you need to build, and how to avoid managing tomorrow's function with yesterday's assumptions.

And if you are simply curious about what AI will do to one of the most foundational functions in business, then the chapters that follow will give you not one answer, but many useful ones.

Because the future of jobs in finance will not be decided by technology alone.

It will be decided by the professionals who see the shift early, build the right capabilities in time, and choose to move from execution to judgment, from reporting to insight, and from function to value.

The old finance professional asked:

Are the numbers right?

The future finance leader will also ask:

What do these numbers mean?

What risk do they hide?

What decision do they demand?

What value do they create?

And what should we do now, before it is too late?

That is the journey this book is about.

PART ONE

Finance Beyond Reporting

Chapter 1

The Steward of Value

JAYESH SANGHRAJKA, CHIEF FINANCIAL OFFICER, INFOSYS LIMITED

There is a certain old-world image of finance that still lives on in many people's minds.

A quiet room.

A serious team.

Files, reports, reconciliations, checklists.

Month-end pressure, quarter-end pressure, year-end pressure.

And a set of people whose primary duty is to make sure that every number lands in the right place.

That image is not entirely wrong.

It is simply incomplete.

Because finance is no longer content to sit in the back office and report what has already happened, and artificial intelligence is accelerating that shift with astonishing speed.

For Jayesh Sanghrajka, CFO of Infosys, the real story of AI in finance is not that machines are taking over. It is that routine work is disappearing, and judgment-driven work is rising to the surface.

The old finance world was built around processing numbers.

The new finance world is being built around shaping decisions.

That is a profound change.

It means finance is no longer defined by the effort it takes to produce information. It is increasingly defined by the quality of insight it brings to the business. What used to take days now takes minutes.

What used to require teams to manually gather, reconcile, and prepare can now be generated at a speed no human setup can match.

And that speed changes expectations.

It changes what leaders ask from finance.

It changes what business teams want from finance.

It changes what a young finance professional must become in order to stay relevant.

In Jayesh Sanghrajka's view, the real future of finance lies not in protecting yesterday's work, but in stepping into tomorrow's role.

A role where judgment matters more than process.

Where trust matters more than transaction.

Where the CFO becomes not merely a controller of outcomes, but a steward of enterprise value.

"AI is stripping finance of routine work and amplifying judgment-driven work."

WHEN FINANCE STOPS COUNTING AND STARTS THINKING

One of the most interesting things about the way Sanghrajka describes the AI shift is that he does not dramatize it as a war between humans and machines.

He doesn't say finance roles are vanishing overnight.

He doesn't say people are becoming irrelevant.

He doesn't even frame it as a threat first.

Instead, he points to a deeper transition.

The work that is mechanical is being stripped away.

The work that is thoughtful is being amplified.

That is a more accurate way to understand what is happening.

For years, finance teams have spent an extraordinary amount of their time doing things that were necessary, but not always high-value. Gathering data, cleaning data, matching entries, reconciling numbers, preparing reports, chasing versions, updating templates, producing analyses that, by the time they were ready, often risked becoming backward-looking.

AI changes the economics of all of that.

When a machine can complete the first layers of analytical effort at speed, the role of finance begins to move upward. Not because someone wrote an inspirational mission statement about it, but because the structure of the work itself has changed.

This is where Sanghrajka's perspective is particularly sharp.

He says, the real change is not fewer finance roles, but more impactful ones.

That one sentence captures the entire dilemma facing the profession.

If you define finance narrowly, then yes, AI looks like a threat.

If you define finance expansively, AI looks like a release.

A release from drudgery.

A release from excessive manual effort.

A release into more meaningful business work.

The question is not whether finance will matter.

The question is: what kind of finance work will matter?

THE WORK THAT IS SHRINKING

The easy part of this transition is naming what is fading.

Sanghrajka identifies the first casualties clearly.

Manual reconciliations.

Report preparation.

Static analysis.

In short, any role that depends heavily on repetitive, data-heavy, rule-based work is vulnerable.

There is no reason to be sentimental about this. The machine is simply better suited for such work. It does not get tired. It does not miss a row in a spreadsheet because it had a long day. It does not wait till Monday morning to process a structured task. It does not confuse one version with another because someone forgot to rename a file.

The danger for finance professionals is assuming that these tasks are still enough to define a career.

For many years, they were.

For many years, organizations still had room for this.

For many years, 'being good with numbers' was treated as if it were a sufficient identity.

It no longer is.

And one can already see why.

If report generation becomes faster and easier, then the report itself loses prestige. The organization starts asking a tougher question: now that we have the report, what do we do with it?

That "what next" question is where the future of finance begins.

Which is why the shrinkage of routine work is not merely an operational issue. It is a philosophical one. It forces finance to re-examine its own sense of self.

Am I here to produce numbers?

Or am I here to improve decisions?

For those who answer the second question well, the profession is opening up.

For those who cling to the first, the walls are closing in.

"Degrees get you shortlisted; skills get you hired and promoted."

THE TALENT THAT IS RISING

Whenever one set of roles shrinks, another rises.

Sanghrajka sees the future belonging to tech-savvy finance partners. Not specialists trapped inside their functional box, but professionals who combine domain depth with analytics, systems thinking, and business storytelling.

That combination is the key.

Finance by itself is no longer enough.

Analytics by itself is no longer enough.

Technology by itself is no longer enough.

The future belongs to hybrids.

A person who understands finance deeply, but cannot work intelligently with data and systems, will soon feel limited.

A person who is excellent with dashboards and tools, but weak in finance judgment, will also stall.

A person who knows both but cannot explain what it all means to the business will struggle to influence.

That is why 'business storytelling' appears in his answer. It may sound like a fashionable phrase, but it points to a very old and very real truth: people do not make decisions from data dumps. They make decisions when somebody helps them understand significance.

The strongest finance professional in the room is not necessarily the one with the most complicated model.

It is often the one who can say, clearly and credibly:

Here is the issue.

Here is what the data suggests.

Here is the risk.

Here is the trade-off.

Here is why this matters now.

This is not a presentation skill alone. It is business thinking.

And then there is systems thinking, another phrase that deserves attention. Systems thinking means understanding not just the number in isolation, but the environment that produced it. It means seeing linkages.

If cash conversion shifts, what does it mean for investment decisions? If a cost line moves, what does it indicate about operating discipline? If a business metric improves, is that real strength, or merely temporary relief?

Machines can point to movement.

Humans must understand what is moving underneath.

That is why the next-generation finance professional will have to be broader, not narrower.

Less clerical.

More interpretive.

Less isolated.

More integrated with the business.

DEGREES OPEN THE DOOR. THEY DO NOT KEEP IT OPEN

Every generation has its own academic comfort blanket.

For some, it was a B.Com.

For others, an MBA.

For others, a professional qualification.

For many families, the belief remains the same: once the right degree is secured, the future is largely settled.

Sanghrajka's answer quietly dismantles that illusion.

Degrees, he says, get you shortlisted. Skills get you hired and promoted.

It is difficult to put it more crisply than that.

The degree still matters, of course. Companies need some marker of discipline, training, and foundation. But the degree is now merely the beginning of the conversation. It is no longer the conclusion.

What differentiates top candidates is not their ability to reproduce textbook content or recite accounting standards from memory. It is how they frame problems, how they use data intelligently, and how they influence decisions.

This is an important distinction.

Traditional finance education often rewards correctness.

Modern finance careers increasingly reward usefulness.

Usefulness means:

Can you understand the business?

Can you think beyond the immediate ask?

Can you use tools without becoming dependent on them?

Can you make sense of data in a messy real-world setting?

Can you hold your own in a conversation where the issue is not accounting treatment alone, but business consequences?

The strongest candidates can do that.

And so, the old academic hierarchy is becoming less reliable as a predictor of future performance. A strong degree helps. It always will. But the market is now watching for something else: evidence of applied thinking.

That is why so many technically brilliant people plateau. They know the subject, but they do not convert knowledge into business relevance.

And that is why some people with fewer glittering academic labels rise fast. They know how to connect knowledge to action.

In finance, that connection is everything.

IS B.COM ENOUGH FOR THE FUTURE?

A great many Indian finance careers have begun with a B.Com degree. It has long been the standard gateway into the profession.

Sanghrajka is respectful, but realistic. B.Com is a good start. It is no longer complete preparation for modern finance roles.

That sentence should be read without defensiveness.

The degree still provides base-level orientation. It is not useless. It is simply insufficient by itself for a world where finance is becoming more analytical, more digital, and more strategic.

He recommends paths that blend finance with analytics, technology, economics, or professional qualifications like CA, CPA, or CMA. That is telling. The future, in his view, belongs not to the one-dimensional finance graduate, but to the person who builds combinations.

Finance plus analytics.

Finance plus systems.

Finance plus economics.

Finance plus professional rigor.

Finance plus continuous upskilling.

That last bit matters the most.

Even the "right" qualification is not enough for a whole career now. No credential can protect a professional from change for very long. The shelf life of static competence is shrinking.

So, the real question for students is not, "Which degree should I do?"

It is, "What kind of finance professional am I building myself into?"

A B.Com degree may still be step one, but the market will ask, very quickly, what came after.

Did you deepen?

Did you specialize?

Did you get digitally fluent?

Did you learn how businesses create value?

Did you become more useful with time?

That is the real exam now.

"Humans will remain essential for judgment calls, ethical decisions, risk ownership, and stakeholder trust."

WHAT AI WILL DO BETTER THAN YOU

Sanghrajka is clear that AI will own data-heavy, repeatable tasks.

Reconciliations.

Variance detection.

Forecasting support.

First-level analysis.

All of these are exactly the kind of work where scale, speed, and pattern recognition matter more than human emotion or contextual subtlety. The more structured the task, the more likely AI will dominate it.

This is not a possibility. It is a trajectory.

And it has two implications.

First, finance teams will become leaner.

Second, the human roles that remain will become more visible.

In the old world, a large team could hide uneven capability. Some people did strategic work, some did operational work, some did repetitive work, and the system somehow carried everyone along. In a leaner, AI-augmented world, each person left standing has to bring more leverage.

One can no longer survive by being "part of the process" if the process itself is being automated.

The machine will not only work faster, but it will also make the old excuses less acceptable.

Why did this take so long?

Why was this not spotted earlier?

Why are we only now seeing this trend?

Why are we spending so much human effort on something that can be automated?

These questions will become more common.

And the finance professionals who feel threatened by them may not actually be threatened by AI.

They may simply be threatened by transparency.

AI exposes low-value work by doing it too well.

That, perhaps, is its harshest gift to the profession.

WHAT AI SHOULD NEVER OWN

If Sanghrajka is clear about what AI will take over, he is equally firm about what must remain human.

Judgment calls.

Ethical decisions.

Risk ownership.

Stakeholder trust.

Each of these deserves a pause.

Judgment calls matter because business decisions are rarely made in fully stable conditions. There are trade-offs, hidden assumptions, timing issues, political overlays, and incomplete information. AI can support this process. It cannot substitute for human discernment.

Ethical decisions matter because just because a choice can be optimized, it does not mean it should be taken. There are values, reputational implications, and questions of fairness that cannot be outsourced to a model.

Risk ownership matters because accountability is not an abstract concept. Someone has to stand behind the decision, defend it, and live with its consequences. AI cannot do that.

Stakeholder trust matters because finance, perhaps more than many other functions, runs on credibility. Investors, boards, auditors, business leaders, regulators, and teams all rely on the perceived integrity of the people in charge. Trust is not built by a perfect dashboard. It is built on responsible human behavior over time.

That is why Sanghrajka's answer goes beyond a technical comment on automation. It is actually a reminder of what finance has always fundamentally been.

Not merely a system of recording numbers.

But a system of trusted stewardship.

If machines take over the mechanics, humans must rise to the stewardship.

That is the bargain.

THE FINANCE TEAM OF THE NEXT DECADE

When Sanghrajka looks ahead ten to fifteen years, the picture he draws is not one of giant finance departments doing larger amounts of work.

It is the opposite.

Finance teams will be leaner.

They will be AI-augmented.

And they will be far more strategic.

This sentence contains all the pressure points for the next generation.

Leaner means there will be less room for passengers.

AI-augmented means working without technological fluency will be difficult.

Far more strategic means, the center of gravity will move upwards.

The finance team of the future will not measure itself by how many reports it produces. It will be measured by how much better the company thought, decided, and allocated because finance was involved.

That is a much more demanding standard.

It requires stronger people.

But perhaps more satisfying work.

The other important shift is that strategy in finance will no longer be limited to planning and budgeting. It will include understanding data governance, AI usage, system reliability, capital allocation, and long-term resilience.

This naturally changes the role of the CFO.

Sanghrajka says the CFO will evolve from a controller of outcomes to a steward of enterprise value.

That phrase is beautiful in its restraint.

He does not say the CFO becomes a celebrity strategist.

He does not say the CFO takes over the business.

He says: steward of enterprise value.

A steward protects, guides, allocates, preserves, strengthens, and thinks in longer arcs.

That, really, is what the modern CFO is becoming.

A steward of value.

A steward of capital.

A steward of trust.

A steward of the company's ability to endure change.

And increasingly, a steward of how data and AI are used inside the enterprise.

This is a much bigger role than finance once held.

But it is also a more exposed one.

Because once you become a steward, you cannot hide behind technical correctness alone. You must exercise judgment.

"The CFO will evolve from a controller of outcomes to a steward of enterprise value."

WHY TRUST WILL MATTER EVEN MORE

Among all the skills Sanghrajka mentions, one quality appears almost quietly at the end, but may turn out to be the most durable of all.

Integrity.

He advises young people to act with integrity and ownership because, in finance, trust and credibility travel faster and last longer than technical skills alone.

That is a powerful line.

We live in a time when technology changes quickly, systems upgrade constantly, AI models improve every quarter, and the half-life of a hard skill can feel painfully short. In such a world, people often chase the next capability, the next tool, the next course, the next certification.

All important.

But some things still compound slowly and last longer.

Trust is one of them.

A finance professional, known to be reliable, fair, thoughtful, and honest, carries a kind of invisible capital. People bring them into harder conversations. They trust them with ambiguity. They believe their judgment. They give weight to their caution. They listen when they say, "This doesn't feel right."

No machine can manufacture that.

Which is why the future of finance, even in its most AI-enabled form, remains a profoundly human profession at the top.

The lower levels may get automated.

The higher levels get humanized.

And that humanization rests on judgment and trust.

THE WINNERS IN THE NEW FINANCE WORLD

Sanghrajka ends with a line that could serve as a motto for the entire future of finance.

The winners will be those who learn continuously and adapt faster than change.

That is not dramatic. It is simply true.

The profession is changing.

The tools are changing.

The pace is changing.

The expectations are changing.

There is no stable plateau to retire on intellectually anymore.

One must keep moving.

And perhaps that is the true story of AI in finance. Not that it replaces humans, but that it removes the hiding places for passive humans. It pushes the profession to become sharper, more integrated, more strategic, and more accountable.

In that sense, AI is not merely disrupting finance.

It is forcing finance to become more itself.

Closer to judgment.

Closer to business.

Closer to stewardship.

Jayesh Sanghrajka's view is neither anxious nor naive. He does not deny the disruption, but he also does not mourn the passing of routine work.

He seems to be pointing finance professionals toward a larger possibility.

Do not compete with the machine where the machine is built to win.

Move where your humanity becomes more valuable.

Into ethics.

Into trust.

Into framing.

Into ownership.

Into value.

That is where the future CFO is already standing.

ADVICE TO YOUNG PROFESSIONALS

Build rock-solid finance fundamentals.

Do not skip the basics in your hurry to sound modern.

Treat degrees as a beginning, not a guarantee.

A good degree opens the door. It does not build a career for you.

Invest early in analytics and technology.

Modern finance will increasingly reward digital fluency.

Learn how businesses create value.

Finance is not only about recording value; it is about understanding how it is made, preserved, and lost.

Develop judgment, not just execution speed.

The machine can process faster. Your edge is in how you decide.

Get comfortable framing problems.

Top candidates stand out by how they think, not only by what they know.

Communicate with clarity.

Insight matters only if others can understand and act on it.

Build credibility deliberately.

In finance, trust compounds over time and becomes a career advantage of its own.

Act with integrity and ownership.

These qualities outlast tools, trends, and technical fashions.

Keep learning.

The winners will be those who adapt faster than change.

Chapter 2

The Value Officer

RAGHURAM KRISHNAN, SR. DIRECTOR & CFO, ADOBE INDIA

There was a time when finance lived at the back of the room.

The numbers were prepared.

The books were closed.

The variance was explained.

The report went out.

And somewhere in the hierarchy of business, finance played the role of the disciplined, dependable adult. Sensible, careful, necessary. But not always central.

That time is ending.

Today, numbers do not wait for month-end. Data does not sit quietly in files. Decisions cannot afford to arrive after the fact. And artificial intelligence, with its speed and scale, is steadily taking away the very tasks that once defined the profession.

In this new world, the old finance identity is no longer enough.

You can see that clearly in the way Raghuram Krishnan talks about his own journey. He does not describe it as a climb through designations; he describes it as a widening of perspective.

The movement, as he puts it, looked like this:

Specialist.

Business Leader.

Decision Influencer.

Executive Partner.

Strategic CFO.

It is a simple sequence, but behind it lies the story of what finance is becoming.

The specialist knows the function.

The business leader understands the business.

The decision influencer shapes choices.

The executive partner sits at the table.

And the strategic CFO sees the enterprise as a whole.

That last leap is the hardest one.

Because it asks finance to stop thinking only in terms of 'my role' and start thinking in terms of 'the company's future'. It asks the finance professional to move from accuracy to insight, from reporting to influence, from control to value creation.

Krishnan calls it becoming an 'enterprise thinker'.

That phrase stayed with me.

Because in just two words, it captures the exact shift that AI is forcing on finance. Machines are getting better at the mechanics of finance. They can process data, identify patterns, produce first-level analysis, and automate repetitive tasks faster than any human team. If finance wants to stay indispensable, it has to move where machines cannot fully go.

Into context.

Into judgment.

Into decision-making.

Into leadership.

That is where Krishnan's story becomes larger than one man's career. It becomes a window into the future of finance itself.

FROM NUMBERS TO NARRATIVE

When people think of a CFO, they usually think of numbers.

Revenue.

Margins.

Costs.

Cash flow.

Forecasts.

Capital allocation.

All true. But that is only the visible layer.

The real evolution, Krishnan suggests, lies in what one does with those numbers.

A finance leader is not merely someone who knows the numbers best. A finance leader is someone who can interpret them, build a narrative around them, and influence strategic decision-making in a way that moves the organization closer to its aspirations.

That is very different from simply "presenting data."

It means understanding what the numbers are saying before the business has fully heard them. It means spotting shifts in patterns, connecting isolated signals, and helping leadership choose between options that may all look reasonable on paper.

In other words, the role has moved from arithmetic to judgment.

And that changes the profile of the person who can succeed in it.

The old image of a finance professional buried in spreadsheets, producing reports, and preserving order, is slowly giving way to a different figure: someone who is commercially alert, analytically strong, technologically comfortable, and able to influence decisions without making noise.

Not the keeper of history.

The interpreter of possibility.

Not the owner of the reports.

The builder of confidence around decisions.

That is a very different kind of finance person.

"Finance is moving from 'number crunching' to 'decision driving'."

THE LEADERSHIP TEST NO ONE TALKS ABOUT

The most revealing parts of Krishnan's response are not actually about AI. They are about what he expects from leaders.

He talks about empowering teams, about letting people take ownership, about not putting them under the bus when things go wrong, about allowing them to fail but helping them see the mistake, correct course, and feel confident enough to take the next decision.

That is not soft leadership. It is demanding leadership.

Because the real challenge is not to create a team that never fails. The real challenge is to create a team that learns faster than it fears.

In finance, this matters more than ever.

If AI is taking away repetitive work, then what remains for people is ambiguity. And ambiguity cannot be handled by frightened teams. It needs teams that can think, decide, and recover. Teams that are willing to try. Teams that know that if they fail honestly, the organization will learn rather than simply punish.

Krishnan's philosophy of leadership has two simple rules.

When you win, take the team along.

When you fail, stand in front.

That is easier to say than to do.

Because in modern corporate life, success is often quietly personalized, and failure is quickly distributed.

But leaders who do the reverse build something rare: trust.

And trust, in an AI-enabled finance world, will become a major source of productivity. A machine may reduce the time needed for analysis, but only a trusted leader can create the courage needed for judgment.

That is why this part of Krishnan's answer is so important. AI may alter the work. Leadership will determine whether the people doing that altered work become more effective or more anxious.

WHAT AI HAS ALREADY CHANGED

The easy thing to say about AI is that it is transforming finance. Everyone says that. The difficult thing is to explain how.

Krishnan's answer is refreshingly specific.

He says the ability to stay on top of the business has improved sharply. Finance teams can now identify patterns and analyze data in ways that simply were not possible within the same timeframe earlier. Insights that once took hours or days can now emerge in seconds or minutes.

That does not just improve efficiency. It changes the timing of relevance.

Finance used to explain what happened.

Now it can shape what happens next.

That is a big deal.

Because if insight arrives too late, it may still be accurate but no longer useful. AI compresses the distance between event and response. It allows the business to see more quickly, act more decisively, and de-risk operations earlier than before.

In a competitive environment, that is not a nice-to-have. It is an advantage.

Krishnan also points to something subtler. AI is helping reduce gaps in language and communication across team members from different backgrounds. This may sound minor. It is not. In large organizations, value is often lost not because people are incompetent, but because they interpret things differently, miss nuance, or fail to communicate consistently.

AI, when used well, can reduce that friction.

It can make teams more coherent.

And coherent teams create better output.

So, the true power of AI in finance is not merely automation. It is acceleration with consistency.

Faster seeing.

Faster learning.

Faster acting.

And with that comes a new standard. Once teams experience this speed, they can never comfortably return to the old cycle of delayed clarity.

THE JOBS THAT WILL FADE

Whenever technology enters a profession, people want reassurance.

Tell me my role is safe.

Tell me the change is gradual.

Tell me adaptation is optional.

Krishnan offers no such comfort.

He is direct about what is at risk.

Pure reporting roles.

Manual data-heavy roles.

Excel-heavy repetitive tasks.

Back-office finance with limited business interaction.

And then he adds something even sharper: average performers who survive by doing routine work and choose not to upskill are also at risk.

That sentence captures the moment finance is in.

For many years, the profession could absorb a broad range of capabilities. There was room for people who were sincere, diligent, and moderately competent at repetitive work. But AI is steadily eroding the economic value of repetition.

If a machine can complete the same task faster, more accurately, and at a lower cost, the organization will eventually stop paying humans to do it.

That does not mean finance jobs will disappear. It means low-leverage finance jobs will.

The danger, then, is not AI.

The danger is standing still while AI climbs your ladder.

There is something almost Darwinian about this phase. Not the strongest will survive. Not the most decorated. The most adaptable.

And adaptability in finance no longer means only learning another accounting standard or another ERP system. It means reimagining your role before the market forces you to.

WHAT THE NEW FINANCE PROFESSIONAL WILL LOOK LIKE

As some roles decline, others grow in importance. Krishnan's list is worth reading, like a hiring blueprint for the next decade.

Business partnering.

Data and analytics thinking.

Tech-savvy finance.

Strategic finance: planning, forecasting, capital allocation.

Storytelling with numbers.

That last phrase is especially revealing.

For years, finance prided itself on objectivity. Storytelling belonged to marketing, leadership, maybe consulting. Not finance.

But anyone who has sat in a management review knows that numbers alone do not move decisions. Someone has to explain what they mean, why they matter, and what action should follow.

The best finance professionals already do this instinctively.

They do not dump numbers.

They frame them.

They do not merely state the variance.

They explain the implications.

They do not leave the leadership team staring at a dashboard.

They point to the decision hidden inside it.

That is storytelling with numbers.

And in an AI world, it becomes more valuable, not less. Because once machines can generate data-rich summaries in abundance, the differentiator shifts to interpretation.

The machine says: Here are the trends.

The human says: Here is what we should do.

That is the new edge.

Tech-savvy finance is also rising because finance can no longer treat systems as somebody else's problem. It does not mean every finance professional must code, but it does mean they must be at ease with analytics, automation tools, AI interfaces, data architecture, and digital workflows.

Likewise, business partnering is no longer a premium add-on. It is becoming central. Finance has to be embedded in functions, not floating above them.

The future finance professional will likely look less like a custodian and more like a commercial navigator.

"AI has no accountability. In situations where outcomes matter, responsibility cannot be delegated to a system."

DEGREES BUILD THE FLOOR. SKILLS BUILD THE CEILING

The debate around degrees versus skills is usually framed too crudely.

As if one must choose.

Krishnan does not.

He says degrees matter. They build the foundation. They matter especially in the early phase of life when formal education gives one structure, peer learning, and breadth of exposure.

But skills are lifelong.

They do not come stamped and sealed at age twenty-one. They keep evolving. They expand or decay, depending on whether one invests in them.

And in the long run, the ability to keep learning, unlearning, and upgrading becomes the true differentiator.

There is a quiet realism in that answer.

Because young people often imagine that the 'right degree' is the decisive event, it isn't. It is only the beginning.

The market does not reward what you once studied as much as it rewards what you can currently do.

In a stable world, the gap between the two may remain manageable. In a fast-changing world, the gap widens quickly.

Finance today is that fast-changing world.

A professional who relies only on the prestige of a past degree will slowly lose relevance. A professional who keeps adding skills becomes future-proof, at least for a while.

And that word "while" matters too. No skill is permanent anymore, which is why learning itself has become the real core skill.

IS B.COM STILL ENOUGH?

For generations of commerce students in India, B.Com was the obvious route into finance. Respectable. Practical. Reliable.

Krishnan sees it as what it is now: a foundation, not a differentiator.

That is perhaps the most honest way to put it.

A B.Com degree still matters. It gives structure, language, and a basic grounding in finance and commerce. But, by itself, it is increasingly not enough for specialized roles.

The market has moved. Employers now seek deeper capability. In many sectors, especially large organizations and IT, there is already a clear preference for postgraduate education, specialized expertise, and practical skill sets that go beyond general commerce.

So, the problem is not with the degree itself. The problem is with stopping there.

The young finance aspirant, who believes a B.Com will automatically open doors, may find the hallway crowded. The one who treats it as a launchpad and keeps building will still have room to grow.

The difference lies in what comes after.

Specialization.

Certification.

Technical fluency.

Practical business understanding.

Communication ability.

Data literacy.

A degree may still get you shortlisted.

But the shortlist is not the career.

That is why the next generation of finance professionals must think less in terms of 'What degree should I get?' and more in terms of 'What stack am I building?'

WHAT AI WILL DO. AND WHAT IT SHOULD NEVER DECIDE

Krishnan's distinction here is one of the most useful in the entire conversation.

AI will increasingly take over binary, rule-based, repetitive tasks. Anything driven by structured data and predefined logic. Data processing, reconciliations, standard reporting, and initial analysis. The machine is built for that.

But the final decision should remain human.

Why?

Because business does not happen in clean, sealed boxes.

A recommendation may make sense statistically and still be wrong strategically. A forecast may look robust but fail to capture a political nuance, a cultural sensitivity, a behavioral reaction, or a one-time market distortion. A capital allocation choice may need to factor in not just efficiency but signaling, timing, and organizational readiness.

Humans, at their best, bring context to the table. They bring memory, intuition, trade-off awareness, and a feel for consequences that no model fully 'owns'.

And then there is accountability.

AI can generate an answer.

It cannot carry the burden of the outcome.

That is why Krishnan insists that AI should remain an enabler, not an authority.

Use it for speed.

Use it for breadth.

Use it to challenge blind spots.

Use it to sharpen your own thinking.

But do not surrender ownership.

In the future of finance, the professionals who thrive will not be those who compete with AI on speed. They will be those who know exactly when to trust AI, when to question it, and when to override it.

THE LEANER TEAM, THE LARGER CFO

If one extends Krishnan's logic into the next ten or fifteen years, a very clear image emerges.

Finance teams will be leaner, heavily tech-enabled, built around a data-first culture, less siloed, and more integrated into the functions they support.

The old model of finance as a central service department pushing information outward will weaken. Finance will increasingly be embedded across the organization. Closer to the action. Closer to decision points. Closer to strategy.

And the people inside those teams will be hybrid.

Not pure accountants.

Not pure analysts.

Not pure technologists.

But combinations.

Finance plus analytics.

Finance plus technology.

Finance plus business understanding.

This hybridization has already begun.

The more interesting shift, however, is at the top.

Krishnan says the CFO will increasingly become a 'Value Officer'.

That is a lovely phrase because it stretches the role without making it vague.

The CFO of the future will still care deeply about control and discipline. But the larger expectation will be this: help the company create value, allocate value, protect value, and explain value.

The CFO becomes a stronger co-pilot to the CEO.

Not the person who merely says yes or no.

The person who says: if this, then that. If we choose this route, here is the implication. If we delay, here is the risk. If we invest, here is the window. If we cut, here is the opportunity cost.

That is not bookkeeping.

That is strategic navigation.

And once finance moves to that altitude, the function is no longer peripheral.

It becomes central to leadership.

THE ADVICE HIDDEN INSIDE THE JOURNEY

Krishnan's advice to students and young professionals is practical enough to be printed and pinned to a wall.

Build a strong foundation. Understand core finance deeply. Do not chase fancy labels without substance underneath.

Invest in skills, not just degrees. Analytics, technology, and communication matter.

Think beyond numbers. Understand how business works, not just how finance reports it.

Stay adaptable. Keep learning, unlearning, and evolving.

Focus on impact. Influence decisions, do not just produce reports.

There is a larger wisdom hidden inside all this.

The future of finance will not reward those who are merely well-qualified. It will reward those who are useful at a higher level.

Useful to teams.

Useful to leaders.

Useful to decisions.

Useful to the business.

And usefulness in modern finance is becoming more human, not less. Not human in the sense of sentiment. Human in the sense of judgment, accountability, context, and communication.

The spreadsheet will survive.

But the person who only knows the spreadsheet may not.

The report will survive.

But the person who only prepares the report may not.

The profession is not disappearing.

It is graduating.

And in that graduation lies both the threat and the opportunity.

ADVICE TO YOUNG PROFESSIONALS

Build the base first.

Know finance concepts deeply before rushing toward niche specializations.

Do not worship degrees alone.

Use them to build a foundation, then keep adding relevant skills.

Learn analytics and technology.

Finance without digital fluency will become limiting very quickly.

Understand business, not just reporting.

The best finance professionals know how the company makes money, spends money, and creates value.

Get comfortable with AI early.

Do not fear it. Learn how to use it intelligently.

Develop judgment.

AI can assist analysis, but accountability will remain human.

Communicate clearly.

If you cannot explain what the numbers mean, you will stay behind the people who can.

Aim to influence.

Do not measure your success only by reports produced, but by decisions improved.

Stay adaptable.

The finance profession is evolving fast, so must you.

Think like an enterprise leader.

That is the path from finance specialist to strategic CFO.

Chapter 3

The Trusted Advisor

NISHANT MOHTA, HEAD OF FINANCE - INDIA, INVESCO

There are some finance careers that begin with a leap.

A dramatic switch.

A bold entrepreneurial plunge.

A sharp break from the known world.

And then, there are careers that are built in a quieter, steadier way.

Qualification by qualification.

Responsibility by responsibility.

Assignment by assignment.

Until one day, without fanfare, the person standing in finance is no longer merely doing finance. He is shaping trust around it.

Nishant Mohta belongs to that second category.

His story is not one of dramatic reinvention. It is one of the professional layering. A finance career built through qualifications, work experience, and a steady willingness to keep expanding capability rather than settling into what had already been achieved.

He began his career in finance after completing Company Secretaryship and Chartered Accountancy. He then grew through experience. At a later stage, he was deployed to the United States and completed the CPA while working there. That, he says, became a turning point.

It did more than add one more credential to his résumé.

It gave him an unusually powerful lens.

He became fluent in both India and US GAAP.

And that changed the trajectory of his career.

From there, his journey moved upward across both product companies and BFSI sector organizations.

What emerges from that progression is a finance leader who believes in the enduring fundamentals of the profession, even as the methods of doing the work are rapidly changing.

For Mohta, the heart of finance remains intact. AI may alter the speed, efficiency, and method of execution, but the core responsibility of finance does not disappear.

Finance, in his view, remains the gatekeeper.

And the trusted advisor to the business.

That is a useful place to begin any conversation about the future of jobs in finance.

Because every few years, a new technology comes along, and the first fear it triggers is this: will the profession itself become unrecognizable?

Mohta's answer is reassuring, but not complacent.

The role will remain.

The way the role is executed will change dramatically.

And those who understand that difference early will be better prepared for the future than those who confuse continuity of purpose with continuity of work.

"The overall responsibility of the finance gatekeeper and trusted advisor of the business will not change."

WHEN A QUALIFICATION BECOMES A TURNING POINT

Many young professionals think of degrees as entry tickets. You study, qualify, get your first role, and then the real game begins.

That is true.

But sometimes, a qualification pursued mid-career becomes much more than a stamp on paper.

It becomes a lens that changes how the market sees you and how you see the profession.

For Mohta, the CPA was one such turning point.

By that stage, he had already built a solid foundation through CS and CA. He was not someone trying to "enter finance." He was already in it, already learning on the job, already moving ahead through experience.

Then came the overseas deployment.

And with it, the chance to step into a wider accounting and reporting universe.

Completing the CPA while working was not simply an academic exercise. It gave him expertise across both Indian and US accounting frameworks. That kind of dual fluency is rare enough to matter and practical enough to alter one's relevance in the marketplace.

One can almost see the career equation shifting there.

From a finance professional to a specialist.

From a specialist to a broader finance leader.

From local capability to cross-market capability.

This is an important reminder for anyone building a career in finance.

Qualifications do not all have equal value at every stage. Sometimes the first degree gets you in, sometimes the next degree shifts your positioning, and sometimes a credential matters less for the technical content and more for the professional credibility and breadth it signals.

That, perhaps, is why Mohta's story feels especially relevant in the AI era.

Because one of the biggest mistakes young professionals make is assuming that once they have one strong qualification, the rest of their career will naturally take care of itself.

It won't.

The future does not belong to the best-qualified person at age twenty-two.

It belongs to the person who keeps strengthening their relevance at thirty-two, forty-two, and beyond.

AI HAS ARRIVED QUIETLY, BUT IT HAS ARRIVED

Mohta does not speak of AI in apocalyptic terms, nor does he pretend it has already reached full maturity.

He sees it as being in an evolutionary stage. There is, in his words, a lot more to come.

That balanced view is perhaps the most sensible one.

Too many people are making one of two mistakes.

Some dismiss AI as overhyped.

Others speak of it as if every finance role will be transformed overnight.

The truth sits somewhere in between.

What is already visible, Mohta points out, is that AI is bringing efficiency to mundane, time consuming work. It is also helping with written communication: drafting emails, preparing formal letters, and making smart summaries of large, complex documents.

This may sound modest compared to grand claims about machine intelligence.

But in everyday organizational life, these are not small gains.

Finance is a profession where time disappears in fragments.

A summary here.

A note there.

An explanation for someone.

A mail to align teams.

A redraft for leadership.

A review of a long document.

A recurring task that no one notices until it takes half the day.

AI's first victory in finance may not be dramatic automation of strategic thinking. It may simply be the quiet reclaiming of time.

Time from low-leverage effort.

Time from repetitive communication.

Time from first-level summarization.

Time from administrative drag.

And once time is reclaimed, expectation changes.

If writing a cleaner email now takes five minutes instead of twenty, then the value of the professional shifts away from drafting toward thinking.

If a dense document can be summarized quickly, the real challenge becomes interpretation.

If process steps can be accelerated, the benchmark for responsiveness goes up.

AI, then, is not merely making finance faster.

It is raising the standard of what finance professionals must now contribute, beyond speed.

THE WORK THAT IS QUIETLY DISAPPEARING

Ask any finance team what consumes time, and the answer often comes not in grand strategic themes, but in ordinary tasks.

Invoice processing.

Payments.

Vendor validations.

Monthly variance checks.

Reconciliations.

Essential work, yes.

Transformative work, no.

Mohta identifies exactly these types of repetitive roles as the ones now in decline.

There is a pattern to all of them.

They are structured.

They are repeatable.

They depend on consistency and logic more than contextual judgment.

And they are often vulnerable to delay, fatigue, and human oversight.

These are ideal targets for AI and automation.

Which means the finance professional, whose role is built mainly around these activities, must start asking difficult questions.

What am I becoming beyond this work?

What do I add when this process gets automated?

What decisions do I help improve?

What understanding do I bring that a machine does not?

The old comfort of repetitive work is eroding, and one can understand why.

If finance talent is still being spent on work that can increasingly be automated, then the organization loses twice over.

It loses time.

And it loses the chance to redeploy human capability into higher-value areas.

That is why Mohta says the roles becoming critical are those that know how to utilize resources like technology and AI to support decision-making.

Notice the shift.

Not technology for its own sake.

Not AI for its own sake.

But using these resources in a way that makes decisions better.

That is a much more mature way of seeing the future.

The machine handles the repetitive.

The professional who can use the machine well rises in importance.

"Roles which were repetitive in nature... are declining. Roles and skills to utilize technology and AI for decision-making are becoming critical."

DEGREES MATTER. COMPLACENCY HURTS

The degrees-versus-skills debate often becomes a slogan battle.

"Skills matter more."

"No, degrees matter more."

"Formal education is outdated."

"No, credentials are everything."

Mohta cuts through this neatly.

Both are equally important.

Degrees help you get your foot in the door. In a competitive world, that still matters. One cannot pretend the screening mechanism has disappeared. Organizations still look at qualifications as signals of discipline, effort, and competence.

But the degree is only the beginning.

The person who becomes complacent after completing a qualification and securing a role will struggle. That is where the real warning lies.

Because complacency in finance is especially dangerous.

It feels respectable.

It feels earned.

It even looks stable from the outside.

A person qualifies well, gets a decent job, performs sincerely, and assumes that progression will naturally follow. But as systems evolve, tools change, and expectations rise, the professional who stops learning gets overtaken not by a more brilliant person necessarily, but by a more curious one.

That is why Mohta emphasizes the need to acquire both technical and soft skills after one has entered the profession.

Technical skills keep you useful.

Soft skills make you scalable.

Without technical depth, one cannot contribute enough.

Without communication, discipline, judgment, and stakeholder management, one cannot lead enough.

The best finance professionals eventually need both.

IS B.COM ENOUGH? THE BLUNT ANSWER

On the question of whether a B.Com degree is enough for a modern finance career, Mohta's answer is direct.

No.

He does not say B.Com has no value. He simply says it is not enough if one wants to move ahead faster and build a stronger finance career. Professional qualifications like CA, CPA, and CMA, in his view, accelerate career progression more meaningfully.

There is a practical realism in this answer.

A B.Com degree can still introduce one to the field. It can create the first layer of accounting and commerce familiarity. But, by itself, it does not create the kind of edge required in a more competitive, more technology-enabled, and more globally benchmarked finance job market.

This is especially true when organizations are looking for people who can handle complexity, compliance, global frameworks, and high-trust finance environments.

The world has moved ahead of generic preparation.

Future finance professionals must think in combinations:

- foundational finance education
- professional qualifications
- practical experience
- technology comfort
- ability to work with data
- ability to communicate with clarity

That is the new stack.

The student who hopes one degree will carry him or her through a forty-year career is likely to be disappointed.

The one who sees each degree as one layer of capability will remain in motion.

WHAT AI CAN DO, AND WHAT IT CANNOT BE TRUSTED WITH

Mohta's division between AI and human work is simple and elegant.

AI will deeply influence repetitive and predictable tasks.

Analytical and decision-making work will still require human judgment.

This distinction is critical because many people confuse analysis with judgment.

The first can often be automated.

The second cannot be fully outsourced.

AI can help detect patterns.

It can compare variances.

It can support forecasting.

It can provide first-level analytical views.

But when the issue becomes: what does this mean for our business, what is the right trade-off, who owns the risk, what consequences are we willing to accept, how should this be communicated, whose confidence is on the line - then human judgment steps back in.

And not just judgment.

Trust.

Responsibility.

Credibility.

These do not sit in software.

A board does not trust a dashboard. It trusts the people who stand behind it. A business leader does not rely only on analysis; they rely on the person whose judgment they believe. A stakeholder does not care merely that a process was automated correctly; they care that someone responsible has applied thought, caution, and fairness where it mattered.

That is why finance will remain deeply human at its most important points.

The lower layers of activity may be automated.

The higher layers of accountability may become even more visible.

AI is not replacing the need for human finance leadership.

It is increasing the need for better human finance leadership.

"Repetitive and predictable tasks will be deeply influenced by AI, and all analytical and decision-making work will require human judgment."

THE CFO OF THE FUTURE WILL STILL BE A TRUSTED ADVISOR

As technology enters finance more deeply, one is tempted to think the role of the CFO itself may become unrecognizable.

Mohta disagrees.

The overall responsibility of finance as gatekeeper and trusted advisor to the business, he says, will not change.

That is a strong statement.

It suggests that while methods, tools, and team structures may shift dramatically, the soul of the CFO role remains intact. The CFO is still expected to protect the integrity of financial stewardship, still expected to be trusted, still expected to guide, and still expected to combine discipline with business understanding.

What will change is how this work gets done.

The finance team, below the CFO, will likely become more automated, more tool-driven, and more analytical in orientation.

The volume of repetitive processing will shrink.

The expectation of responsiveness will rise. More will be known more quickly.

More can be explained faster. More scenarios can be generated with less manual effort.

This will not reduce the need for CFOs.

It will increase the standard for what good CFOs must now be.

A trusted advisor in the future will need to understand not only finance, but the enabling systems behind finance.

Not only policy, but digital process.

Not only accounting logic, but also how AI-supported workflows shape insight and risk.

The CFO's authority, then, will rest on a wider base.

Still gatekeeper.

Still advisor.

But operating in a much more transformed environment.

There is something steadying in this thought.

Professions often change by changing their tools first and their identity later. Mohta's view suggests that finance has begun changing its tools rapidly, while its deeper purpose remains surprisingly stable.

Perhaps that is why the profession will survive AI better than some fear.

Its deepest value was never only in processing.

It was in trust.

THE VIRTUES THAT NEVER GO OUT OF FASHION

At the end of his response, Mohta offers just three words of advice.

Commitment.

Hard work.

Discipline.

At first glance, they may sound old-fashioned in a world obsessed with AI, analytics, digital transformation, and future-ready capability.

But perhaps that is exactly why they matter.

Technology changes fast.

Human seriousness still matters slowly.

Commitment means staying with the work long enough to build mastery.

Hard work means doing the unglamorous effort that still lies behind most excellence.

Discipline means not becoming careless in a profession where trust is built on consistency.

One can layer analytics on top of that.

One can add AI tools, strategic thinking, and systems fluency.

But without these old virtues, the structure remains weak.

There is also a deeper truth hidden here.

People often imagine that the future belongs only to those who know the newest tools.

That is only partly true.

The future belongs to those who can combine new tools with durable personal qualities.

A disciplined person learns AI better.

A committed person keeps reskilling.

A hardworking person closes the gap faster than the lazy one who has access to the same tools.

So, perhaps Mohta's final answer is not simple at all.

It is just fundamental.

And fundamentals, in finance as in life, have a way of returning.

WHAT THIS MEANS FOR THE YOUNG FINANCE PROFESSIONAL

If one were to draw the larger lesson from Mohta's perspective, it would be this:

Do not mistake the automation of tasks for the decline of the profession.

Finance is not shrinking in importance.

It is shifting in shape.

The repetitive layers are thinning.

The judgment layers are thickening.

The gatekeeping role remains.

The trusted advisor role remains.

But the route to becoming that advisor is changing.

The future finance professional must, therefore, be prepared in three ways.

First, technically.

Second, digitally.

Third, personally.

Technically, because finance fundamentals still matter.

Digitally, because tools and AI will increasingly shape the work.

Personally, because trust, discipline, and credibility remain non-negotiable.

Nishant Mohta's own journey reflects all three.

He built qualification.

He built relevance.

He widened his lens.

And he kept going beyond the first milestone.

That may well be the most practical lesson of all.

The future of jobs in finance will not belong to those who merely enter the field.

It will belong to those who keep becoming larger than the role they first entered with.

ADVICE TO YOUNG PROFESSIONALS

Get the basics right.

Build a strong base in finance before chasing shortcuts or fancy labels.

Respect degrees, but don't stop at them.

Qualifications help you enter. Growth depends on what you build after that.

Do not become complacent.

The degree that got you your first role will not guarantee your long-term progression.

Add professional depth.

Qualifications like CA, CPA, or CMA can significantly strengthen and accelerate your finance career.

Learn how to use technology and AI.

The future belongs to those who can work with these tools, not ignore them.

Move toward decision-support work.

Repetitive tasks will decline.

Judgment-oriented finance work will rise.

Build soft skills along with technical skills.

Communication, clarity, maturity, and stakeholder confidence are critical in finance leadership.

Value discipline.

In finance, consistency and trust are built slowly and lost quickly.

Stay committed.

Career growth is not built in one qualification or one promotion, but over years of effort.

Remember the essence of finance.

The tools may change, but finance will remain the gatekeeper and trusted advisor to the business.

PART TWO

Inside the New Finance Engine

Chapter 4

The Hybrid Accountant

SHRENIK SHAH, MANAGING DIRECTOR,
ARMANINO INDIA LLP

For a long time, accounting was seen as the most dependable of professions.

Orderly.

Precise.

Process-driven.

Built on rules, checklists, and deadlines.

The work was hard, no doubt, but the path seemed clear.

You learned the standards.

You mastered the numbers.

You built accuracy.

And over time, you earned trust.

But now, the profession is standing at a turning point.

The old accounting engine was built to process history.

The new one is being rebuilt to interpret the future.

And artificial intelligence is speeding up that transition.

For Shrenik Shah, Managing Director at Armanino India LLP, the shift is unmistakable. Over the next decade, he believes accounting will move from being transaction-driven to insight-driven. The repetitive work at the core of the function - bookkeeping, reconciliations, basic compliance, sampling-based audit routines - will increasingly be handled by AI-enabled systems and integrated platforms.

What remains for humans will be more valuable, but also more demanding.

Less data preparation.

More data interpretation.

Less execution.

More orchestration.

Less routine processing.

More business partnership.

In that world, the accountant does not disappear.

But the old version of the accountant does.

"Accountants will move from being processors of historical data to strategic business partners."

FROM TECHNICAL PROFESSIONAL TO STRATEGIC LEADER

Some careers are built on one core strength, sharpened over time. Others grow by widening the circle of responsibility.

Shrenik Shah's journey belongs to the second category.

He began in the accounting and advisory space, building the classic base of the profession: tax compliance, financial discipline, and client servicing. Those are the skills that teach a young professional two things very quickly. First, that details matter. Second, that trust is earned, not by intention, but by consistency.

But over time, his role began to change.

He moved into leadership positions where the work was no longer only about technical correctness. It became about scaling teams, improving operations, setting up processes, and contributing to larger growth initiatives. He was no longer simply producing work. He was creating the system through which work could be produced well by others.

That is an important threshold in any finance or accounting career.

The professional starts by mastering the task.

The leader begins when he must design the machine around the task.

A key turning point in Shah's journey came through people and organizational leadership, especially in scaling teams and aligning India operations with global standards. His experience with international firms also gave him exposure to cross-cultural collaboration, particularly between the United States and India.

That experience matters a great deal in modern accounting.

Because accounting is not just technical anymore. In global firms, it is also cultural. Work moves across geographies. Processes are shared across teams. Reporting expectations differ by jurisdiction. Clients expect consistency, but teams may think, communicate, and execute differently depending on where they are based.

The leader who can bridge that gap becomes more than technically sound. He becomes structurally useful.

In his present role, one of Shah's major responsibilities has been expanding the India practice, with a strong focus on hiring, high-performance teams, and stronger internal processes.

That phrase, "people, process, and growth", appears almost quietly in his response. But it says a lot.

Because AI may reshape accounting tools.

But organizations are still built by people.

Scaled by process.

And sustained by growth discipline.

In that sense, Shah's own journey mirrors the future of the profession. He began in technical accounting, grew into operational leadership, and now speaks about a future in which accounting itself must combine domain expertise with systems, data, and business thinking.

WHEN ACCOUNTING STOPS LOOKING BACKWARD

Traditional accounting has always had a deep relationship with the past.

What happened?

What was earned?

What was spent?

What was owed?

What was recorded correctly?

What was missed?

That backward-looking discipline remains essential, but Shah believes the center of gravity is shifting.

The accounting function, especially in the U.S. context, is moving from transaction-driven to insight-driven.

This is one of the most important changes underway.

In the old model, accounting teams processed transactions and ensured correctness. In the new model, much of the transaction layer will increasingly be automated. AI-enabled systems and integrated ERPs will handle a large share of bookkeeping, reconciliations, and baseline compliance.

That does not make accounting less important.

It makes old accounting less central.

The work that rises in its place is richer.

Advisory and decision support.

Real-time insights.

Forecasting.

Scenario planning.

Risk management.

Governance around automated outputs.

System oversight.

This is a much larger role than accounting once occupied.

It asks accounting professionals to understand not just what the numbers are, but what the business should learn from them. It pushes them closer to management decisions. And it requires a new kind of confidence, the confidence not merely to report information, but to interpret it.

There is also a subtle but significant shift in the sequence here.

Earlier, data had to be prepared before it could be discussed.

Now, AI can help generate and organize data much faster.

So the premium moves to interpretation.

That is why Shah says the future belongs to people who can tell the story behind the data, not merely produce the data itself.

And once storytelling enters accounting, the profession changes in temperament.

The best accountants of the future will still be careful.

But they will also need to be commercially expressive.

"The role of finance professionals will evolve toward data interpretation and storytelling, rather than data preparation."

THE JOBS THAT WILL SHRINK

Every profession has its clerical heart.

The tasks that no one glorifies, but everyone depends on. The work that is repetitive, structured, and necessary. For decades, accounting has had many such roles.

Shah lists them out with clarity.

Manual bookkeeping and data entry roles.

Basic AP and AR processing roles.

Junior audit roles focused on sampling and tick-and-tie work.

Compliance-only tax preparers with no advisory angle.

These are the first places where AI and automation will cut deepest.

It is easy to see why.

This work is high in volume, low in ambiguity, and based on known rules. AI systems thrive in such environments. They can process faster, flag deviations, maintain consistency, and scale in a way human teams cannot.

For young professionals, this has one major implication.

It is no longer enough to enter the profession through the lowest-value, repetitive layer and assume one will naturally rise with time. In the past, a person might spend years building a career through repetitive accounting work, slowly learning the system and moving up. That ladder is becoming less dependable.

The bottom rungs are being redesigned.

This is not a reason for panic, but it is a reason for clarity.

The profession still needs people.

It simply needs fewer people for repetitive work and more people for interpretive work.

And that changes how one should prepare from the beginning.

THE NEW ROLES EMERGING INSIDE ACCOUNTING

If old roles are shrinking, what exactly is replacing them?

Shah's answer is one of the most concrete roadmaps in this book.

He sees strong demand emerging for:

AI-enabled accountants and finance analysts, who can interpret system outputs

Data analytics specialists within accounting, using tools like Power BI and SQL

Automation and process transformation lead

AI governance and controls specialists

Strategic finance and FP&A professionals

Client advisory professionals who can combine accounting knowledge with industry insight.

This is a striking list because it shows how accounting is fusing with three adjacent worlds:

- technology
- analytics
- business advisory

That fusion is the future.

The accountant who only knows accounting will remain employable, perhaps, but increasingly boxed in. The accountant who knows how to read data, understand systems, manage automation, and advise clients at a business level will rise faster.

And then there is a new and particularly interesting category: AI governance and controls.

This is the kind of role that did not exist in old accounting.

As AI systems do more of the work, someone must ensure the outputs are reliable, auditable, explainable, and compliant. The old accounting instinct for control, documentation, and skepticism does not disappear here. In fact, it becomes newly valuable.

That is worth underlining.

Technology does not kill the accounting mindset.

It repurposes it.

The same caution that once went into manual checking may now go into AI oversight. The same concern for auditability may now apply to automated workflows. The same professional skepticism may now be directed toward AI-generated outputs.

In that sense, the profession is not abandoning its old DNA. It is redeploying it into a new ecosystem.

"The opportunity will shift toward professionals who can combine accounting expertise with technology, analytics, and business acumen."

THE SKILLS THAT WILL MATTER MOST

Shah's answer on skills is both practical and forward-looking.

He says success in accounting's new landscape will depend on three broad things:

- technical expertise
- technology fluency
- business mindset

That is the new triangle.

Without technical depth, one cannot remain credible.

Without technology fluency, one cannot remain efficient.

Without a business mindset, one cannot remain relevant.

He goes further and identifies key capabilities:

data literacy and analytics

technology fluency across ERP systems, RPA, and AI tools

critical thinking and professional skepticism

- business acumen

communication and storytelling

process improvement mindset

This list deserves careful reading because it reveals how much the profession is shifting.

Data literacy means understanding what data says and does not say.

Technology fluency means being comfortable with systems, not intimidated by them.

Professional skepticism becomes even more important when AI outputs look polished.

Business acumen means knowing the 'why' behind the number.

Storytelling means helping management act on financial insight.

Process improvement means never assuming the current workflow is the best one.

And then there are the mindsets.

Adaptability.

Continuous learning.

Curiosity.

Ownership.

Accountability.

These sound almost generic until one places them in the context of AI.

When machines do more of the visible work, humans are left with the parts that require posture.

How alert are you?

How willing are you to learn?

How much responsibility do you take for the output, even when part of it was machine-generated?

This is where accounting becomes less about precision alone and more about maturity.

The future accountant will not only need to know more.

He or she will need to relate differently to work itself.

IS B.COM ENOUGH? NOT ANYMORE

There was a time when a traditional commerce degree could sustain a long and respectable accounting career.

That time has passed.

Shah is clear on this. A degree like B.Com is a good foundation, but not sufficient on its own in today's environment.

That is a realistic answer, and an increasingly common one.

Foundational degrees still matter. They provide vocabulary, structure, and entry-level familiarity. But accounting today sits at the intersection of global standards, digital systems, data tools, automation, and advisory expectations. A plain degree, by itself, cannot prepare a professional fully for that world.

Shah recommends a layered path.

First, core professional qualifications:

CPA for U.S. accounting and global firms

CA or ACCA, depending on direction

Second, technology and analytics learning:

- advanced Excel
- Power BI or Tableau

basic SQL or practical data handling,

exposure to automation tools

familiarity with AI tools in accounting,

Third, continuous learning through structured programs, online platforms, and internal firm-led certification.

Fourth, practical exposure:

Real client work, process improvement projects, automation initiatives.

This is one of the clearest educational blueprints any student of accounting could ask for.

The message is simple.

Degrees may get you in the door.

But long-term success depends on continuous upskilling, especially at the intersection of accounting, analytics, and technology.

That intersection is where the profession is heading.

And that is where serious professionals must head, too.

WHEN AI STOPS BEING A TOOL AND STARTS BECOMING A TEAMMATE

One of the most compelling parts of Shah's response is his mention of agentic AI.

Most people still imagine AI as a helper, a summarizer, a copilot, a faster calculator.

Shah is already thinking one step ahead.

He describes agentic AI as systems that can independently perform multi-step tasks, interact, and make decisions within defined boundaries. In the context of accounting, that means AI is not just automating one small piece of a workflow. It is beginning to execute an end-to-end sequence.

That is a very important shift.

He gives examples:

- reading emails
- extracting invoices
- posting entries
- reconciling accounts
- reviewing vendor communication
- validating invoices
- following up on collections
- drafting responses
- helping in audits through anomaly detection and document verification
- gathering tax data from multiple systems
- preparing draft returns

coordinating financial close tasks

even handling basic client interactions

This is no longer "automation" in the old sense.

This is delegated execution.

Or, as Shah puts it beautifully, agentic AI can act like a junior team member.

That line captures the moment accounting is entering.

Not machines replacing all humans.

Not humans merely using machines.

But professionals managing a hybrid workforce in which some members are digital.

That is a profound shift in professional identity.

The future accountant may not only supervise staff.

He or she may increasingly direct workflows carried out by AI agents.

Work changes from doing the task to reviewing, directing, and governing the task.

"Professionals become orchestrators of AI agents, not just executors."

WHAT MUST REMAIN HUMAN

Even with all this automation, Shah is equally clear about what stays firmly in human hands.

Final decision-making and sign-offs.

Financial statements.

Audit opinions.

Tax positions.

Complex accounting judgments.

Revenue recognition.

Estimates.

Policy interpretation.

Advisory and business partnering.

Client relationship management.

Exception handling.

Ethics, governance, and AI oversight.

That list reads like the surviving core of professional accounting.

And for good reason.

Because all of these involve one or more of the following:

- interpretation under ambiguity
- context sensitivity
- consequence-bearing choices
- trust-based relationships
- accountability
- ethics

AI can support these areas. It can even improve them, but it cannot fully own them.

A model can flag unusual revenue patterns.

But recognizing what that means in a complex commercial arrangement still needs judgment.

A system can draft a response to a client.

But trust is not built through draft quality alone. It is built through empathy, credibility, and context.

An AI tool can process tax data.

But taking a position still requires professional courage and accountability.

This is where accounting remains stubbornly human.

And perhaps that is why the profession, even as it transforms, will not disappear. It will simply move upward.

Less clerical.

More judgmental.

Less repetitive.

More relational.

Less mechanical.

More strategic.

THE FUTURE ACCOUNTANT

By the end of Shah's response, one can see the shape of the future accountant quite clearly.

Not a bookkeeper in the traditional sense.

Not a pure compliance machine.

Not merely a preparer of statements.

But a hybrid professional.

One who understands accounting deeply.

Uses technology fluently.

Interprets data intelligently.

Questions outputs critically.

Explains implications clearly.

Improves processes continuously.

And partners with the business strategically.

This accountant does not fear AI.

He or she directs it.

This accountant does not define value by the volume of work done.

But by the quality of insight provided.

This accountant does not cling to the old romance of manual effort.

But respects the new leverage of digital systems without surrendering professional skepticism.

That is, perhaps, the most mature vision of all.

A profession transformed, but not diminished.

Rebuilt, but still recognizable.

Modernized, but still anchored in trust.

ADVICE TO YOUNG PROFESSIONALS

Build a strong technical base.

Accounting, audit, tax, and finance fundamentals still matter deeply.

Get professionally qualified.

Certifications like CPA, CA, or ACCA add real credibility and open global opportunities.

Do not stop at accounting.

Layer your profile with analytics, systems understanding, and technology fluency.

Become comfortable with tools early.

Advanced Excel, Power BI, dashboards, basic SQL, and automation tools will increasingly matter.

Use AI before it uses your job.

Start applying AI in your daily work so you become more productive, not more vulnerable.

Learn to understand the "why."

Do not just pass entries or complete tasks. Understand business impact.

Develop communication and advisory skills.

Your career growth will depend on how well you explain insight, not just on how well you prepare reports.

Be curious and keep learning.

Even one hour a week of structured learning compounds over time.

Think of your future identity differently.

Aim to become a problem solver who understands finance, leverages technology, and influences business decisions, not just an accountant.

Chapter 5

The Continuous Auditor

BALAJI RANGANATHAN, SENIOR AUDIT DIRECTOR, WELLS FARGO

There was a time when audit moved to a familiar rhythm.

You planned the review.

You selected the sample.

You asked for documents.

You tested controls.

You wrote observations.

You closed the file.

Audit, in that world, was periodic by design.

It looked backward.

It worked in cycles.

It relied on samples because there was simply no practical way to look at everything.

And much of its craft lay in disciplined execution.

That world is now changing.

And few professionals are better placed to see that change than Balaji Ranganathan, who spent nearly two decades in external audit before moving into internal audit, where he has spent the last fifteen years. It is a career that has seen both sides of assurance: the formal discipline of external review and the embedded, institution-facing reality of internal audit.

If one had to summarize his perspective in a single line, it would be this:

Audit is moving from periodic, sample-based, and retrospective to continuous, risk-sensing, and insight-driven.

That is not a cosmetic shift. It is a change in the operating logic of the function itself.

And AI is one of the biggest reasons.

Ranganathan does not believe AI will replace auditors, but he is equally clear that it will change what auditors examine, how they examine it, and where human judgment truly matters.

That is, perhaps the most useful way to think about the future of audit.

Not as a profession under extinction.

But as a profession under redesign.

The old tools made a certain kind of audit necessary.

The new tools make a different kind of audit possible.

And once the possible changes, the standard changes too.

"AI won't replace auditors, but it will fundamentally change what we audit, how we audit, and where human judgment adds the most value."

TWO DECADES OUTSIDE, FIFTEEN YEARS INSIDE

Some careers gain strength through depth in one system, while others gain unusual value through contrast.

Balaji Ranganathan's journey carries that contrast.

He spent almost two decades in external audit before transitioning into internal audit. That is not merely a change in employer category or reporting structure. It is a shift in vantage point.

External audit trains you in discipline, evidence, standards, and formal assurance boundaries. It teaches professional distance. It teaches you what it means to examine with rigor while remaining independent of the management process.

Internal audit, especially over the long run, teaches something else. It places you closer to the organization's living risks. It gives you visibility into how controls behave in motion, not only at reporting points. It pushes you to understand systems, decisions, incentives, emerging issues, and the institutional context around risk.

Ranganathan says the last fifteen years in internal audit have been an amazing journey, one that reinforced the value of perspective, adaptability, and continuous learning.

Those three words are revealing.

Perspective, because internal audit increasingly requires seeing risk not just in a checklist, but in business reality.

Adaptability, because no two environments stay stable for long.

Continuous learning, because the risk landscape itself keeps evolving.

That progression also gives weight to his comments on AI.

He is not reacting from the outside. He is speaking as someone who has watched audit evolve over decades and who knows the difference between a passing efficiency tool and a structural shift in the profession.

For him, AI is clearly the latter.

FROM SAMPLE-BASED TO SIGNAL-BASED

Audit has always lived with a practical limitation.

You cannot test everything.

So you test enough to form a view.

That is why the sample-based audit became standard. It was a sensible response to human and technological limits. You selected a subset, reviewed documents, performed procedures, and drew conclusions with professional judgment.

But AI begins to change the logic behind those limits.

When far larger volumes of data can be scanned, compared, pattern-matched, and monitored continuously, the old dependence on periodic sampling becomes less central. It does not disappear at once, but it loses its monopoly as the primary mechanism of assurance.

This is what Ranganathan means when he says internal audit will become continuous, risk-sensing, and insight-driven.

Continuous means audit activity is no longer confined to occasional review windows.

Risk-sensing means the function gets closer to live signals, anomalies, patterns, and emerging control issues.

Insight-driven means value lies less in the fact of testing and more in the meaning extracted from what is being observed.

That is a major shift.

Because once an audit moves closer to continuity, it also moves closer to management relevance. Issues can be identified earlier. Trends can be sensed before they harden into control failures. Attention can move from historical confirmation toward future-facing risk awareness.

In that sense, AI does not merely make audits faster.

It changes its timing.

And timing changes influence.

An audit insight that arrives after the event is useful.

An audit signal that arrives while corrective action is still possible is far more powerful.

"Internal Audit will move from being periodic, sample-based, and retrospective to being continuous, risk-sensing, and insight-driven."

THE WORK THAT WILL SHRINK

Ranganathan is very specific about the roles that will decline.

Manual, sample-based testing.

Document-heavy coordination.

Execution layers built around repetitive audit mechanics.

These are the functions that AI is naturally positioned to absorb.

Much of audit has historically depended on gathering, reviewing, comparing, tracking, and documenting. Necessary work, yes. But often labor-intensive and process-heavy. AI can increasingly automate elements of that execution, making audits faster, more consistent, and more scalable.

This is especially true for:

- planning support
- data analysis
- control testing
- issue tracking
- reporting mechanics

That phrase, "reporting mechanics", is important. In many functions, people confuse the production of a report with the creation of insight. AI will widen that difference dramatically.

The mechanics of audit may become easier.

The judgment inside the audit will become more visible.

And that visibility may unsettle many traditional role structures.

For years, junior audit roles were built partly around repetitive execution: sampling, tick-and-tie style procedures, document follow-up, and evidence organization. This work served both the function and the apprenticeship model of the profession.

As those tasks get automated, the profession must rethink not just staffing but learning. How will younger auditors build judgment if the repetitive layers that once trained them become thinner?

This is one of the most serious long-term questions for audit as a profession.

The work may disappear.

But the developmental function of that work must somehow be replaced.

THE ROLES THAT WILL GROW

If old audit work thins out, what replaces it?

Ranganathan points to three major directions.

AI-augmented auditors.

Continuous risk analytics.

AI governance and model risk assurance roles.

That list is significant because it tells us that audit is not simply becoming more digital. It is becoming more hybrid.

The future auditor will not only understand controls and procedures, but they will also increasingly need to understand how AI-supported systems behave, where they can fail, and how their outputs should be challenged.

The AI-augmented auditor is not someone replaced by machines, but someone who uses AI to widen audit coverage, sharpen issue identification, and deepen risk interpretation.

Continuous risk analytics means audit teams must become more comfortable reading dynamic signals rather than static files. They will need to understand patterns, thresholds, anomalies, behavioral indicators, and system-generated insights as part of routine audit work.

And then there is AI governance and model risk assurance, a role category that is likely to grow sharply.

As organizations rely more on models, automated workflows, and AI-generated recommendations, someone must test not just controls in the old sense, but the reliability, explainability, governance, and risk implications of these systems. Audit is naturally positioned to play a part here, but only if its people evolve.

That is the pattern one sees, again and again, in the future of finance and assurance professions.

The old discipline does not become irrelevant.

It gets redirected toward new sources of risk.

Professional skepticism does not vanish.

It acquires a new target.

"New opportunities will grow around AI-augmented auditors, continuous risk analytics, and AI governance/model risk assurance roles."

WHAT THE FUTURE AUDITOR MUST LEARN

Ranganathan's answer on future capability is one of the clearest in the entire set of responses.

He names five elements that will matter:

- judgment
- critical thinking
- the ability to interpret AI-driven insights
- data literacy

understanding of AI risks and governance

And then he adds something equally important: a learning mindset.

That combination is exactly right for internal audit.

Judgment matters because an audit cannot become a mechanical reading of AI output. Someone must decide what the signal means, what the risk is, and how strongly the issue should be framed.

Critical thinking matters because AI systems can produce polished outputs that create a dangerous illusion of certainty. An auditor who stops questioning because the system looks intelligent ceases to be an auditor in the deepest sense.

Interpretation matters because AI-generated patterns are not audit conclusions by themselves. They are prompts, inputs, and signals. Human professionals must still translate them into meaningful risk judgments.

Data literacy matters because audit teams will increasingly need to understand how data is structured, what its limitations are, and what confidence they can place in machine-generated analysis.

And understanding AI risk and governance matters because the function itself must evolve to oversee the systems the business is increasingly depending upon.

Above all, the learning mindset matters because every one of these areas will keep changing. No single training program or one-time certification can solve for the next twenty years. The auditor of the future must become comfortable learning alongside technology rather than waiting to be trained after the fact.

That is a large cultural shift.

Audit has traditionally respected discipline and consistency.

Now it must also reward intellectual agility.

IS B.COM ENOUGH? ONLY AS A START

On the question of educational preparedness, Ranganathan is balanced but clear.

A traditional degree like B.Com is still a good foundation.

But it is no longer sufficient on its own.

This is becoming a recurring theme across the book, but it takes on a specific shape in audit.

Because audit now sits at the intersection of:

- financial understanding
- risk assessment
- process comprehension
- data analysis
- technology awareness
- AI and model governance

A plain commerce degree can introduce one to the language of accounting and business. But, by itself, it cannot fully prepare a professional for a world where assurance increasingly involves automated systems, live data, AI-supported processes, and emerging forms of non-financial risk.

Ranganathan recommends combining core qualifications like CA, CPA, or CIA with data literacy, AI awareness, and technology-risk learning.

That stack is worth noting.

CA, CPA, CIA: the old pillars of professional credibility.

Data literacy: the new working language.

AI awareness: the new field of relevance.

Technology risk understanding: the new assurance frontier.

The most striking phrase in his answer, however, is this: treat learning as an ongoing capability, not a one-time credential.

That is, perhaps the right educational philosophy for the AI age.

The degree gets you started.

The profession now expects you to keep rebuilding yourself.

"What differentiates professionals today is continuous learning."

WHAT AI CAN AUTOMATE IN AUDIT

Ranganathan offers one of the most useful practical descriptions of AI's role in audit.

It will increasingly automate:

- planning support
- data analysis
- control testing
- issue tracking
- reporting mechanics

This matters because it clarifies that AI's impact on audit is not just about one tool or one process. It is spread across the lifecycle of an audit.

Planning support means AI can help shape the scope, surface data patterns, and prepare first-level inputs.

Data analysis means it can process volumes of evidence no manual team could handle efficiently.

Control testing means repetitive execution can be accelerated.

Issue tracking means audit follow-ups can become more systematic and visible.

Reporting mechanics mean the effort of assembling output declines.

The result is not that the audit becomes less serious.

It becomes less burdened by mechanics.

But he is equally careful not to overstate the machine's authority.

What continues to require humans, he says, is:

- judgment
- professional skepticism
- ethical reasoning
- stakeholder judgment

translating AI insights into meaningful risk conclusions, especially in areas that are complex, emerging, or ambiguous.

That final clause is important.

Complex.

Emerging.

Ambiguous.

Those are exactly the kinds of risks that keep leaders awake at night, and they are also the zones where mature audit professionals will continue to matter most.

Machines are best where patterns are known.

Humans are best where meaning is still forming.

THE FUTURE OF INTERNAL AUDIT

If one listens carefully to Ranganathan's answer, the future internal audit function starts to take shape.

It will be less periodic.

Less sample-dependent.

Less document-heavy.

Less procedural in its visible form.

And more:

- continuous
- analytical
- technology-enabled
- risk sensitive

- judgment-heavy

The internal auditor of the future may spend less time "doing" low-level procedures and more time understanding where the business is vulnerable, where AI-generated insights point, and how to convert machine-supported analysis into credible, useful assurance.

This also means the function may become more strategically useful to management, provided it evolves fast enough. A continuous, risk-sensing audit function can become an early-warning mechanism, rather than merely a post-facto reviewer.

That is a bigger role.

But also a more demanding one.

Because once the internal audit gets closer to strategic relevance, it must develop stronger capability in communication, risk framing, and organizational influence.

The days when one could survive in audit through process discipline alone are fading.

Process discipline will remain necessary.

It will no longer be enough.

WHAT BALAJI RANGANATHAN'S VIEW REALLY TELLS US

There is something quietly serious about the way Ranganathan sees the future.

He does not romanticize the old audit world.

He does not panic about AI either.

Instead, he seems to be saying: this is a profession built on judgment. If AI removes repetitive mechanics, then judgment becomes even more important, not less.

That is a powerful thought.

Because the future of audit, and perhaps much of finance, may not lie in preserving older forms of effort, it may lie in protecting and strengthening the qualities that only become visible when routine work is stripped away.

Professional skepticism.

Ethical reasoning.

Stakeholder judgment.

Interpretive clarity.

Accountability.

These were always part of the audit.

AI is simply making it impossible to hide behind processes.

And that may be the true redesign of the profession.

ADVICE TO YOUNG PROFESSIONALS

Build strong audit fundamentals early.

The basics of assurance, risk, and control still matter deeply.

Do not stop with traditional audit knowledge.

Layer your profile with data literacy, AI awareness, and technology-risk understanding.

Treat learning as a continuous capability.

In audit, what keeps changing is not just tools, but the risk landscape itself.

Develop judgment and critical thinking.

The machine may support execution, but risk conclusions still need mature human interpretation.

Protect professional skepticism.

AI-generated output should sharpen questioning, not replace it.

Strengthen communication.

The value of audit lies not only in identifying issues, but in helping others understand their significance.

Stay curious about technology.

You do not need to become a technologist, but you do need to understand the systems shaping modern risk.

Hold on to integrity.

In audit, credibility still compounds slowly and matters immensely.

Remember where the profession is heading.

From periodic and retrospective to continuous and risk-sensing, from sample-based assurance to insight-driven audit.

Footnote:

The views expressed are personal and do not represent those of the author's current or former employers.

Chapter 6

The Finance Engineer

VISH DHINGRA, PARTNER, BIG 4

Autonomous accounting will redraw the controller's role and redefine the CFO's mandate. Vish Dhingra, Partner at a Big 4 Consulting firm argues that the finance professionals who endure will look less like bookkeepers and more like 'finance engineers' - and that the transition has already begun.

A feature, informed by the work of Vish Dhingra, Partner at a Big 4 Consulting firm. (the views expressed in this book are solely those of the author in his personal capacity and do not represent the views of any organisation with which the author is or has been affiliated)

EXECUTIVE SUMMARY

Most forecasts about finance and technology are largely focused on costs, a faster close, a cheaper shared-services centre, a lower finance-to-revenue ratio. The argument advanced here is different in kind. Within eight to ten years, the finance function will not merely be cheaper or faster - it will be structurally unrecognisable. The key driver of this revolutionary change is the advent of autonomous accounting: AI agents that execute meaningful portions of the accounting and reporting lifecycle within defined controls, rather than tools that simply accelerate individual efficiency.

The strategic consequence is larger than efficiency. For a century, finance has been constrained by a single bottleneck: producing the numbers consumed most of the capacity that might have been spent interpreting them. Autonomous execution dissolves that constraint, and in doing so completes finance's long migration from scorekeeper to strategist - from recording what happened to shaping what happens next. The CFO becomes less a steward of reporting and more an orchestrator of enterprise performance, equipped with real-time, predictive, and increasingly prescriptive intelligence.

This transition reorders the function's architecture - its operating model, its metrics, its talent, and its risks. The traditional accountant who refuses to embrace technology will find their role shrinking. The future belongs to what Vish calls the techno-functional "finance engineer" - someone who designs, governs, and improves technology-driven finance processes instead of merely operating them..

The opportunity and the danger sit close together. Autonomous workflows scale good design - and bad design - at machine speed, making governance, explainability, and trust the new sources of competitive advantage. The organisations that win will not be those that automate first, they will be those that redesign the function around a deliberate new division of roles between human judgment and machine execution.

I. A CLAIM WORTH TAKING LITERALLY

Most predictions about technology and the finance function are mostly about cost. They promise a leaner close, a cheaper service centre, a point or two shaved off the cost of finance as a share of revenue. Vish is making a different kind of claim, and finance leaders should treat it as such. The function will not be recognisable within eight to ten years. Not cheaper. Not faster. Unrecognisable.

For an audience that has absorbed a decade of automation promises, the reflex is to negate this like others. That would be a mistake. Vish has spent more than three decades in professional services advising clients across more than a dozen countries, leading large teams of finance professionals and developing technology solutions to transform finance functions. He is not narrating disruption from the outside; he has spent his career inside the plumbing of finance, where the work actually happens and where it actually breaks.

"The finance function won't be recognisable in the next eight to ten years."

The change underway is architectural, not cosmetic. That it alters not just the speed of the work but the operating model, the metrics, the talent, and the risk profile of the function simultaneously. That is precisely the change Vish describes - and it begins with a shift the profession has been promising itself for thirty years and never fully delivered.

II. FROM SCOREKEEPER TO STRATEGIST - FINALLY

Finance has spent a generation trying to move from recording the past to shaping the future: from scorekeeper to business partner, from reporting to insight. The ambition is old. The results have been uneven, and the reason is structural rather than cultural. Producing the numbers has always consumed the capacity that might have been spent interpreting them. Close cycles, reconciliations, consolidations, and controls absorbed the very people whose judgment the business most needed. The function was busy being accurate about yesterday.

Autonomous accounting attacks that constraint directly. When agents collect and validate data, reconcile accounts, highlight exceptions, and assemble first-draft reporting, the scarce human resource - analytical judgment - is freed from production and redirected toward interpretation, foresight, and decision support. This is what turns a familiar slogan into a genuine inflection point. The migration from scorekeeper to strategist stops being an aspiration competing with the close, and becomes the natural use of newly liberated capacity.

The destination is what might be called decision intelligence: finance as the enterprise's real-time sensing and steering system. Reporting that once arrived monthly and backward-looking becomes continuous and forward-leaning. Variance analysis gives way to predictive signalling - not only what the margin was, but where it is heading and why. The most advanced finance organizations will move further still, toward prescriptive guidance: not merely flagging a working-capital problem, but proposing and modelling the corrective actions and quantifying their trade-offs. In that world the CFO is no longer the custodian of the rear-view mirror. The role becomes that of an orchestrator of enterprise performance, sitting at the centre of the company's data and translating it into the decisions that determine where value is created and destroyed.

III. THE INFLECTION POINT BENEATH THE SURFACE

A function evolves continuously, but it rarely reaches an inflection point. That point, in Vish's framing, comes when the old assumptions stop holding - and finance is nearing it. You can tell because four things shift at once.

Operating models change because work is no longer organized solely around human teams executing process steps; AI agents become part of the operating fabric, and the unit of design shifts from the team to the human-machine system.

Metrics change because headcount-and-throughput measures of finance productivity lose their meaning when software executes at scale; the function must learn to measure value created, insights delivered, control quality, exception management, and decision impact.

Roles change because people are no longer hired chiefly to process, reconcile, and report, but to understand the systems, data, controls, and business outcomes those activities serve.

And risk changes because autonomous and agentic systems introduce exposures the profession has never had to govern at scale: incorrect execution, model drift, opacity, governance gaps, automation bias, and control failures that propagate at machine speed.

This is the substance behind the word unrecognizable. The masthead on the function will still read "finance." The mechanics underneath will not be the ones today's leaders were trained to manage.

IV. AUTONOMOUS ACCOUNTING: THE ENGINE OF THE SHIFT

For years, "finance automation" meant accelerating a single process — a workflow tool here, an ERP configuration there, a bot for a repetitive step, a dashboard to cut manual reporting. Autonomous accounting is categorically larger. It describes a controllership function in which AI agents execute significant portions of the accounting lifecycle on their own, inside defined rules, controls, and governance boundaries: collecting and validating data, processing transactions, performing reconciliations, identifying exceptions, triggering downstream workflows, drafting reports, supporting the close, flagging anomalies, coordinating across systems, and maintaining their own audit trails.

"Autonomous accounting will be the future of the finance controllership function."

The decisive feature is not that any one of these tasks is automated - many already are - but that they begin to chain together into self-executing workflows, with the human role shifting decisively upward. People design the process.

They define the intended outcomes. They interpret the outputs and study the anomalies. They make the decisions the data points toward. The agents execute the rest.

That is a different controllership model, and a different controller. The controller of the future may supervise not a large team performing manual work, but a hybrid system of people, platforms, and autonomous agents. The job tilts away from managing effort and toward governing execution — a change that sounds like a relief and is in fact a heavier responsibility. If an agent posts, reconciles, and acts, someone must still validate that it is acting correctly, calibrate its thresholds, monitor its exceptions, and ensure it is not optimizing the wrong objective with quiet precision. Someone must understand how a single machine-made error can replicate across thousands of transactions before a human notices. This is why, in Vish's account, the future finance professional cannot simply be comfortable with AI. They must know how to design around it.

V. THE NEW GEOMETRY OF THE FINANCE WORKFORCE

Every architectural shift redraws the talent map, and Vish is unusually direct about who is exposed. The pure-play traditional accountants who do not embed technology, data, and AI in their day's work - will find their roles gradually narrowing.

"Pure-play traditional accountants who do not embrace tech, data, and AI will find their roles gradually narrowing."

This is not a dismissal of accounting; it is a warning about stagnation. Technical accounting knowledge still matters, but it no longer stands alone. The professional who says - "I know the numbers, but technology is not my area," is making a quietly dangerous career bet. That separation was once defensible - technology specialists sat elsewhere, and accountants could be users of systems rather than thinkers about them. As accounting itself becomes something executed by technology-enabled agents, the division collapses. Few accountants need to become software engineers, but all of them need enough fluency to interrogate an output, trace a data flow, and contribute to redesigning a process. Those who refuse will not vanish overnight; their relevance will simply narrow, and in a fast-moving market a narrowing relevance is usually where decline begins.

Who advances in their place? Vish's answer is the techno-functional finance engineer — neither a finance expert nor a technologist, but a hybrid who designs finance outcomes. The "techno-functional" half denotes genuine command of both the subject matter and the technology that transforms it; the "finance engineer" half denotes the ability to design, automate, govern, and rethink finance processes rather than merely operate inside them. Their distinctive value is translation: the capacity to sit with a technology team without getting lost and with a finance team without being superficial, connecting process, data, system, and outcome. The finance function of the future will be built neither by accountants alone nor by technologists alone, but by people who can bridge the two.

That capability will open a spread of roles carrying different titles across companies but resting on the same foundation - finance, plus technology, plus judgment: finance process architects, autonomous-accounting designers, AI-enabled controllership specialists, data-led transformation leaders, and finance AI governance professionals. For finance leaders, the immediate implication is a workforce strategy problem, not merely a hiring one. The pipeline that produced the last generation of controllers will not produce the next, and the talent cannot simply be bought in a market where every function is competing for the same hybrid profile. It must be deliberately built.

VI. THE CAPABILITY STACK - AND THE CLASSROOM PROBLEM

The skill set Vish prescribes is short and demanding, and conspicuously more rigorous than the standard exhortation to "be digital." It runs: technology and data science; AI engineering; critical thinking and logical reasoning; mathematical deduction; and deep subject-matter expertise. Each earns its place.

Data science, because finance will run through data-rich, system-mediated environments, and a professional must understand how data is captured, structured, and interpreted.

AI engineering, because AI is migrating from a surface-level productivity aid to something embedded in the process - and embedded systems must be designed, governed, and improved, not merely used.

Critical thinking, because AI now produces outputs faster than any human can manually verify them, placing a premium on the ability to detect a weak assumption or a flawed conclusion.

Mathematical reasoning, because data-driven finance is ultimately about patterns, probabilities, and inference, not dashboards.

Subject-matter depth, because technology without domain understanding is not transformation but fragility: a professional may master the tool and still misread the accounting, the risk, or the business consequence.

The implications reach upstream of the workplace, into how the profession is educated. Traditional degrees, though extremely important, will no longer suffice on their own; subject matter knowledge has to be braided together with technology skills. An accounting major should pair the degree with a data science minor. Every degree, in his view, should carry a data or technology component.

"An accounting major should also study a data science minor."

The point lands hardest against the way curricula are still organised - accounting in one box, analytics in another, strategy in a third - when real finance problems no longer respect those boundaries. A single issue today may fold together accounting treatment, ERP configuration, data quality, AI-generated analysis, regulatory exposure, process design, and model risk. A professional trained in only one dimension cannot lead the whole conversation. For employers, this is not a problem to be outsourced to universities and professional bodies. Finance and technology skills go out of date so quickly these days that how a firm trains its own people has become a real source of competitive advantage.

VII. GOVERNANCE, TRUST, AND ACCOUNTABILITY AT MACHINE SPEED

Every large gain in productivity arrives with a governance bill attached, and autonomous finance presents an unusually steep one. The efficiency is real; so is the risk, and the risk compounds. A human error is typically contained. An agent's error, repeated across a high-volume workflow, multiplies before anyone notices - and the more reliable the system appears, the less likely a human is to be watching when it fails.

The hard questions are not peripheral; they determine whether autonomous accounting can be trusted at all. Who owns a decision an agent has executed in part? How is a self-executing workflow audited, and how is its reasoning made explainable to a regulator or an audit committee? How are controls built around systems that learn and adapt? How is bias prevented, and how is trust preserved when fewer human hands touch the process directly? These are the questions, Vish suggests, where consulting, risk, controllership, and technology increasingly converge - and where a distinct professional opportunity is opening for those who can not only use AI but govern it.

The strategic reframing here matters. In an autonomous function, trust ceases to be a compliance overhead and becomes a source of advantage. The organisation that can demonstrate to its board, its auditors, and its regulators that its autonomous processes are controlled, explainable, and accountable will move faster and deploy more aggressively than the competitor that cannot - because it will be permitted to. Governance, properly built, is not the brake on autonomous finance. It is the licence to operate it at scale.

This is also why the human role in Vish's future of finance is anything but passive. Professionals will do less manual execution and far more architecture; less production, more oversight; less preparation, more interpretation. That makes the role more leveraged but also more accountable. If an agent executes a poorly designed process, the failure is still human. If the intended outcome is badly defined, the automation will faithfully scale the wrong goal. If a persuasive dashboard is accepted without scrutiny, the accountability does not transfer to the dashboard. The discipline is not "let AI do everything." It is "design the system through which AI does the right things" - a brief that calls for stronger professionals, not weaker ones.

VIII. THE WIDENING GAP BETWEEN LEADERS AND LAGGARDS

If the destination is broadly shared, the pace and quality of arrival will not be. The same technology that promises a strategic finance function also raises the cost of getting it wrong, and the gap between leading and lagging finance organisations is likely to widen into a chasm along several lines.

The first is data. Autonomous workflows are only as trustworthy as the data they run on; an agent reconciling against fragmented, low-quality data will industrialise error rather than insights. The organisations that have treated data as a strategic asset - governed, structured, and owned - will compound their advantage, while those that deferred the unglamorous work of data foundations will find that no quantity of AI compensates for it.

The second is operating-model courage. Bolting agents onto an unchanged process yields a faster version of the old function and little more. The genuine value comes from redesigning the work around the new division of labour - and that requires leaders willing to dismantle structures, roles, and metrics that have defined finance careers for decades.

The third is talent, where the advantage flows to organisations that begin building the techno-functional "finance engineers" bench now, before the market for it tightens further.

And the fourth is trust, where the firms that invest early in governance and explainability will earn the freedom to scale autonomy while more cautious or more reckless rivals stall.

What unites these is a single underlying convergence: finance, technology, and business strategy are ceasing to be separable domains. The finance function becomes a competitive instrument precisely where those three meet - and the leaders of the next decade will be the ones who stop managing them as separate disciplines.

IX. THE DECADE AHEAD

Strip away the vocabulary and the argument is unusually unhedged. Finance will be structurally transformed. Autonomous accounting will redefine controllership. Accountants who avoid technology will fade. The finance engineer will rise. None of it will be secured by bolting a few tools onto old processes; it will require rethinking operating models, metrics, talent, education, and risk governance together.

The professional who emerges is a demanding composite - part accountant, part technologist, part analyst, part process designer, part risk thinker, part business adviser. It is a harder persona to build than the narrow accountant of the past, and a far more powerful one. The same is true of the function itself. The finance organisation that arrives at the end of this transition will be smaller in headcount but larger in influence, less occupied with producing the numbers and more central to the decisions the numbers inform.

The machine, in the end, will execute. The finance engineer - and the CFO who builds the institution around that figure - will design, govern, and decide. That division of labour is where the disruption hides its real opportunity, and it will not wait for the organisations that hesitate to claim it.

IMPLICATIONS FOR FINANCE LEADERS

For CFOs, controllers, and boards weighing what to do with this, the agenda resolves into a handful of decisions that cannot be delegated:

Treat this as redesign, not automation. The value is not in making the existing process faster; it is in re-architecting the function around a deliberate division of labour between human judgment and machine execution. Automating an unexamined process simply scales it.

Reset the metrics before the technology. Productivity measures built on volume and headcount will mislead in an autonomous function. Define now how you will measure insight, control quality, exception management, and decision impact — or you will optimise for the wrong outcomes at speed.

Make data foundations a board-level priority. Autonomous workflows industrialise whatever data they are given, including its flaws. Data quality, ownership, and governance are no longer IT housekeeping; they are the precondition for trustworthy autonomy.

Build the techno-functional bench deliberately. The hybrid finance engineer cannot be bought at scale in a contested market. Invest in reskilling, redesign career paths, and treat the firm's learning architecture as competitive infrastructure.

Make governance a source of advantage, not a brake. Invest early in controls, explainability, and accountability for autonomous processes. The organisations that can prove their systems are trustworthy will be licensed to scale them; those that cannot will stall - or fail loudly.

Locate accountability with humans, explicitly. Decide in advance who owns the outcome of an agent's actions, how autonomous workflows are audited, and where the human checkpoints sit. Accountability does not transfer to the machine, however capable it becomes.

Lead the convergence personally. Finance, technology, and strategy are merging into one domain. The CFOs who manage them as separate disciplines will be outpaced by those who recognise that the finance function is becoming the enterprise's decision-intelligence engine - and lead it as such.

Chapter 7

The AI-Ready Finance Leader

VIVEK C, HEAD OF FINANCE, TECHNOLOGY SECTOR

There was a time when a strong finance team was judged by discipline.

Did the books close on time?

Were the numbers accurate?

Was the reporting clean?

Did the controls hold?

Those things still matter. They always will.

But they are no longer enough.

The finance function is now entering a phase where efficiency will not come only from process improvement, shared services, or stronger systems. It will come from something larger. From artificial intelligence moving into everyday work. Not as a side tool. Not as an experiment. But as part of the operating fabric of finance itself.

Vivek C sees that future very clearly.

He began in the world of the Big Four audit, working with large manufacturing businesses such as the Tata Group. From there, he moved into the technology sector, managed finance responsibilities across different regions within APAC, and later led major controllership responsibilities, including setting up teams in India as part of a record-to-report transformation journey.

That background matters.

Because it gives him a view of finance across both traditional and modern operating models, he has seen the old discipline-heavy world of audit and manufacturing finance. He has also seen the highly scaled, technology-driven finance environment where digital capability is no longer optional.

So, when he says AI is at the core of future efficiency, it is not a fashionable comment. It is a practical conclusion from years spent inside evolving finance systems.

In his view, finance teams will be significantly different in the years ahead. Mundane accounting work will be disrupted. Recurring tasks will be automated. Basic data gathering and analysis will happen faster and more accurately through AI. And the real differentiator in hiring will not simply be finance knowledge, but the ability to use AI effectively in day-to-day work.

That is a major shift.

For a long time, finance rewarded accuracy first.

Now, it will increasingly reward intelligent leverage.

Not just who knows the process.

But who can redesign the process around AI.

"AI is the core of all future enhancements."

FROM AUDIT TO APAC TO AI

Some careers build depth through one domain, while others build range by moving across contexts.

Vivek C's journey seems to have done both.

He started in Big Four audit, in a setting that usually teaches the core disciplines of finance early and well: rigor, structure, consistency, control, and respect for process. Auditing large manufacturing companies is one of the best ways to understand the bones of a business. You see working capital, costs, inventory, controls, reporting, and governance in a very grounded way.

Then he moved into the technology sector.

That shift alone is significant.

Manufacturing finance and technology finance do not merely differ in sector economics. They differ in speed, systems intensity, operating model, and the pace of business decision-making. A person who moves successfully between them learns not just finance, but adaptability.

He then went on to manage different regions within APAC, widening the frame further. Regional finance leadership teaches a professional how similar finance principles play out across different business settings, teams, expectations, and levels of maturity. It also teaches scale.

One turning point, he says, was leading APAC controllership in his previous organization and setting up teams in India as part of a record-to-report transformation.

That is an important clue to how he sees the future.

Transformation experience changes a finance leader's mindset. Once you have built teams, redesigned processes, and moved work into new structures, you stop seeing finance as a static function. You start seeing it as something that can be rebuilt, reconfigured, and modernized.

That mindset is especially relevant in the AI era.

Because the finance leaders who will navigate this shift best are not those who only know how to run the current model well, they are the ones who know how to change the model itself.

WHEN AI STOPS BEING OPTIONAL

A lot of companies still talk about AI as if it were an initiative.

A pilot here.

A workshop there.

A few use cases identified.

Some internal experimentation.

Vivek's answer suggests that this phase will not last long.

AI, he says, is at the core of all future enhancements.

That means something important: the future finance function will not ask, "Should we use AI?" It will ask, "How well are we using AI already?"

This is a big shift in posture.

In earlier waves of digital transformation, companies could delay adoption without immediately feeling left behind. With AI, that luxury may not last. The speed and quality gains in areas like analysis, information retrieval, summarization, recurring workflow execution, and reporting support are already significant enough that they will start influencing how leaders evaluate finance teams.

That is why Vivek links AI directly to efficiency.

Not abstractly. Not in theory.

He is talking about finance teams that can gather data faster, analyze existing information more quickly, and improve the day-to-day rhythm of work by using AI tools intelligently.

And in a technology-led environment, that expectation becomes even stronger. Once AI becomes widely available, the bar moves.

The question is no longer whether the task can be done.

It is how quickly, how accurately, and how intelligently it can be done.

That changes the benchmark for individual professionals as well.

The person who works hard without AI may still be respected.

The person who works smart with AI will be more scalable.

"Basic accounting, data gathering, and analysis can be done much faster and more accurately with AI."

THE WORK THAT WILL DISAPPEAR FIRST

Vivek is clear that mundane and low-end accounting roles will be disrupted first.

That makes sense.

All professions have an invisible layer of repetitive work beneath the surface. In finance, that includes recurring accounting activity, routine data gathering, initial analysis, repetitive review steps, and mechanical reporting preparation.

These tasks are essential in the present model, but they are also exactly the kind of work AI can absorb well.

This is not just about automation in the narrow sense. It is about the changing economics of attention.

If AI can retrieve the information, organize it, compare it, draft the first output, and support analysis, then the human professional is no longer needed for the act of production alone. The human is needed for interpretation, supervision, exception handling, decision support, and governance.

That means the old career ladder changes.

Traditionally, many professionals entered finance through repetitive work. They learned by doing month after month of process-heavy tasks, gradually understanding the larger system. But if the repetitive layers shrink, the profession must rethink how people build early-career capability.

That is not a reason to fear AI.

It is a reason to become larger than repetitive work early.

The professional who defines himself or herself by task execution alone will find it hard to stand out. The professional who uses task automation as a springboard toward higher-value contribution will rise faster.

This is where finance starts separating into two tracks.

One track keeps asking: How do I preserve my current work?

The other asks: What new work becomes possible once current work is automated?

The future belongs to the second track.

THE NEW HIRING SIGNAL

One of Vivek's strongest points is that future hiring will increasingly value people who understand AI and can implement AI tools from a user perspective.

That last part matters.

Not everyone needs to be a model builder.

Not everyone needs to code.

But finance professionals must be able to work with AI practically.

This means:

- understanding where AI can save time
- knowing how to structure questions and prompts
- using AI for analysis and summarization
- evaluating output quality
- integrating AI into workflows
- spotting where AI is useful and where it is not
- making teams more efficient through actual usage, not mere awareness

This user-perspective capability may become a major hiring differentiator.

Because companies do not need only AI theorists, they need professionals who can put AI to work in the flow of real operations.

That is why the future finance candidate will be judged not only by finance knowledge, but by digital behavior.

Do they use tools intelligently?

Can they improve the quality of their work with AI?

Do they understand how to supervise automated output?

Can they move from information access to better decision support?

These are practical questions, and hiring will increasingly move in that direction.

Finance knowledge remains necessary.

But operational AI fluency may become the new multiplier.

"Someone who could implement AI tools from a user perspective is going to be a critical skill for future hiring."

DEGREES STILL MATTER, BUT THEY NO LONGER LEAD ALONE

Vivek does not dismiss degrees. In fact, he says a degree is still critical to provide the right background for the role.

That is an important point. In many discussions about the future of work, people swing too far in the other direction and pretend that foundational education has lost all relevance. It hasn't.

Finance still requires conceptual understanding.

Accounting logic still matters.

Professional discipline still matters.

The language of business still matters.

A degree helps build that base.

But Vivek's real emphasis lies elsewhere. AI skill, he says, will be more critical going forward. Candidates will increasingly be expected to implement AI in day-to-day work and become more efficient through it.

That is a meaningful shift in the hierarchy of employability.

Earlier, the degree was the main proof.

Now the degree becomes a foundation, while AI-enabled execution becomes the differentiator.

This is similar to what is happening across knowledge professions. Employers no longer only ask: What have you studied? They are increasingly asking: what can you do with today's tools, in today's environment, against today's productivity expectations?

And that means the old separation between 'knowledge' and 'work style' is weakening.

The future candidate will need both:

- a good conceptual base
- visible ability to use AI effectively

That is why Vivek recommends not only graduation, but stronger professional qualifications, such as CA, CPA, or CMA, depending on the function, combined with AI capability.

This combination is likely to become the new premium profile.

Deep finance understanding.

Recognized qualification.

Practical AI usage.

Decision-oriented output.

IS GRADUATION ENOUGH? NOT REALLY

Vivek's answer here is practical and straightforward.

Graduation alone may not be enough. Someone with CA, CPA, or CMA, depending on the finance function, combined with AI skills, would be highly desirable.

That sentence captures how the future of finance talent will likely be assessed.

The base degree may still get a candidate into consideration, but higher professional qualifications show deeper seriousness and technical maturity. In a competitive market, they still matter.

What changes is that these qualifications, by themselves, will not be enough either.

They need to be paired with the ability to function effectively in an AI-enabled environment.

That means the future finance professional may need to think in layers:

- foundational education
- professional qualification
- AI tool fluency
- analytical ability
- presentation and decision-support capability

The person who builds only the first two layers may still find work. The person who builds all five will have far more leverage.

This is a useful way for students to think.

Do not ask only: which degree should I pursue?

Ask also: what work profile am I preparing myself for?

Because the market is no longer hiring only a finance graduate, it is hiring a finance professional who can operate in a transformed function.

"Graduation may not be enough; someone with CA/CPA/CMA with AI skills would be highly desirable."

WHAT AI WILL AUTOMATE. AND WHAT IT WON'T

Vivek's distinction here is both precise and realistic.

All recurring tasks and tasks that rely on existing information can increasingly be automated.

This is an important formulation.

A large amount of finance work is built on recurring cycles and known data. Close activities, periodic reports, standard reconciliations, operating checks, recurring summaries, base-level analysis, comparisons, and presentations often draw heavily on existing information. AI is naturally suited to such work.

Once the information exists, AI can:

- retrieve it quickly
- summarize it
- compare it
- draft output
- flag patterns
- produce first-level analysis.

That means the human role moves elsewhere.

Vivek says there will still be a degree of supervision required to ensure AI tools are providing accurate and quality output, and are being used in the best way possible.

That is an understated but crucial point.

AI does not remove the need for quality control.

It changes where quality control sits.

The professional of the future will not just do the work. He or she will increasingly supervise the system doing the work.

That requires:

- understanding what "good output" looks like
- spotting hallucinations or shallow reasoning
- validating that the AI used the right context

- ensuring the output is decision-useful
- checking whether efficiency came at the cost of precision
- governing use, so that tools are used thoughtfully rather than lazily

So, the human role is not simply 'above' AI. It is also 'around' AI.

Around its assumptions.

Around its use.

Around its quality.

Around its consequences.

And that is why finance will not become less human at the top. It may become more human in the parts that matter most: judgment, review, governance, and meaningful decision support.

THE FINANCE TEAM OF THE FUTURE

Vivek is clear that finance teams will be significantly different in the future.

Their success, he says, will depend on the successful adoption of AI. Day-to-day functioning itself will require AI tools.

This is one of the strongest operational statements in the set of responses you have collected.

It means AI will not be reserved for high-profile transformation projects or a handful of innovation champions. It will become woven into everyday finance work.

If that happens, then the finance team of the future will look different in at least four ways.

First, it will likely be leaner in terms of repetitive execution work.

Second, it will be more tool-dependent, in the sense that effective functioning will require daily interaction with AI-supported systems.

Third, team capability will depend not only on financial competence, but on adoption quality. Two finance teams with similar technical strength may perform very differently, depending on how intelligently they use AI.

Fourth, the boundary between "doing" and "reviewing" will shift.

Professionals will spend more time supervising, validating, interpreting, and presenting than manually producing.

This also changes leadership.

A CFO or Head of Finance will no longer only manage the function in a traditional sense. They will need to ensure the function is actually AI-capable. That means adoption, training, behavior change, governance, and productivity standards become part of finance leadership itself.

The finance leader of tomorrow will not just ask:

Are the numbers right?

They will also ask:

Are we using AI well?

Are we using it safely?

Are we getting real leverage from it?

Are our people becoming stronger because of it, or more dependent in the wrong way?

That is a new leadership brief.

And it is already beginning.

"The success of finance teams would depend on the successful adoption of AI."

THE NEW RESPONSIBILITY OF THE CFO

One of Vivek's most practical insights is about the changing role of the CFO.

CFOs, he says, will still manage finance as a function. But they will also have to ensure that their teams are efficient in the use of AI.

This sounds simple. It is not.

Because it means the CFO's job expands beyond finance stewardship into capability stewardship.

Not only:

- closing books
- ensuring controls

- supporting decisions
- managing teams

But also:

- ensuring adoption of the right tools
- building AI fluency across the finance organization,
- defining standards for use
- creating efficiency without losing quality
- ensuring finance talent evolves with the function

This is a major transition.

The CFO of the future will not merely be the most senior finance professional in the room. He or she may increasingly become the architect of a hybrid finance system, one in which people and AI tools work together every day.

That changes what leadership means.

In the past, finance leadership could rely heavily on process discipline and technical review. In the future, it will also require transformation management: how to get teams to work differently, think differently, and create value differently.

That is why finance leadership is becoming as much about capability design as about financial oversight.

WHAT STUDENTS SHOULD REALLY DO NOW

- Vivek's advice to students and young professionals is unusually practical.

He tells them to have a fresh perspective about their careers and actively gather experience with AI tools through training and on-the-job exposure.

That is exactly right.

Young professionals often wait for the market to fully clarify before acting, but by the time the market clarifies, the early movers already have an advantage.

The right approach now is not passive awareness. It is hands-on familiarity.

Learn how AI tools work.

Use them in real tasks.

Understand where they help and where they fail.

Build comfort early.

Vivek also makes another crucial point: because so much information is now available through a simple AI query, the future skill is not access to information. It is using the information well.

This may be one of the most important transitions of the AI era.

Information used to be scarce.

Now it is abundant.

So the premium moves to selection, analysis, interpretation, and presentation.

That is where future professionals must focus.

Not just finding answers.

But shaping useful output for decision-making and governance.

This is especially relevant in finance.

The best finance professional will not be the one who merely retrieves the data fastest. It will be the one who can analyze it properly, present it clearly, and support governance and decision-making in the most effective way.

That is a much more valuable role.

And one far less likely to be commoditized.

WHAT VIVEK C'S VIEW REALLY MEANS

There is a practical seriousness in Vivek's response.

He does not romanticize old finance work.

He does not overcomplicate the future either.

His basic point is clear:

AI will automate recurring work.

Finance teams will have to use AI daily.

Future hiring will value practical AI implementation ability.

Degrees will remain relevant, but AI-enabled execution will matter more.

The role of finance leadership will expand into AI capability-building.

That is a coherent and defensible picture.

It suggests that the future of finance will not be won by professionals who merely know the rules. It will be won by those who can combine finance depth with digital fluency and use AI to strengthen decision support and governance.

The spreadsheet is not disappearing.

The finance professional who only knows the spreadsheet may.

The function remains.

The operating model changes.

And in that change lies both the threat and the opportunity.

The people who begin adapting now will likely have the strongest platform later. The people who postpone adaptation until AI becomes unavoidable may find that, by then, the job has already changed around them.

That is the real warning in Vivek's response.

Do not wait for certainty.

Build relevance early.

ADVICE TO YOUNG PROFESSIONALS

Build a strong finance base.

Core knowledge still matters, and professional qualifications remain valuable.

Do not stop at degrees.

Graduation alone may not be enough for future finance roles.

Add AI skills early.

Practical familiarity with AI tools will increasingly matter in hiring and performance.

Learn by doing.

Training helps, but on-the-job experimentation matters more.

Focus on how to use information, not just how to find it.

AI makes information easy to access. Your value lies in analysis, interpretation, and presentation.

Develop decision-support capability.

The future finance professional will need to help business leaders act, not just report.

Understand governance.

AI-led efficiency is useful only if the output is accurate, high-quality, and used properly.

Stay open-minded about your career.

The future function will look different. Build toward where it is going, not where it was.

Adopt a fresh perspective.

AI is not just a new tool. It is changing the nature of the work itself.

PART THREE

The Human Edge

Chapter 8

The Curious CFO

TEJASWINI RAJWADE, CFO, TECHNOLOGY SECTOR

Some finance careers are built like straight highways.

A degree.

A role.

A promotion.

Another role.

A bigger title.

A bigger team.

And then, one day, the CFO's chair.

But some careers are built differently.

They are built through movement.

Across functions.

Across geographies.

Across kinds of business problems.

Across situations that stretch not just technical competence, but managerial character.

Tejaswini Rajwade belongs to that second kind.

She describes her journey as one that has unfolded over more than three decades, across multiple geographies and diverse roles. Not a narrow climb inside one box called finance, but a broad-based build-out of financial, operational, and strategic capability. A journey designed, consciously or unconsciously, to prepare her not merely to manage numbers, but to lead large enterprises.

That distinction matters.

Because the modern CFO is no longer simply the most senior finance person in the building, the role has outgrown that definition. In many companies, finance now sits at the nerve center of business decision-making. It influences capital, risk, growth, control, transformation, talent, and increasingly, technology itself. The CFO is expected to know not just what the numbers are, but what they mean, how they connect, what they hide, and what the business should do next.

And now AI has entered the picture.

For most professions, AI arrives as an outsider.

For finance, it arrives like a natural extension.

Because finance, at its core, runs on data.

And wherever there is data, there is pattern.

Wherever there is pattern, there is automation.

And wherever there is automation, there is a redefinition of human work.

That is the world Tejaswini Rajwade is describing.

A world in which finance is being reshaped not at the margins, but from the inside out.

"Finance is based on data. And with hygienic data, roles that needed crunching, parsing, and insights can all be run by AI."

THREE DECADES TO SEE THE WHOLE PICTURE

There is a certain confidence that only long careers can produce.

Not the loud confidence of someone who wants to impress you.

But the calm confidence of someone who has seen enough cycles to know what really changes, and what merely looks new.

Tejaswini's journey stretches across more than thirty years, and what stands out in that journey is not a single dramatic turning point, but the deliberate accumulation of breadth.

Multiple geographies.

Diverse roles.

Financial depth.

Operational exposure.

Strategic leadership.

This kind of career build is important because finance leadership at the top is rarely the result of accounting expertise alone. Many people know finance. Far fewer know business. Fewer still know how businesses behave across markets, systems, and cultures.

And that is often what separates a strong finance executive from a true CFO.

A CFO must understand operations well enough to know where performance gets created or destroyed.

Must understand strategy well enough to know which numbers matter before they are visible.

Must understand organizations well enough to know how decisions travel through power, process, and people.

That kind of perspective is rarely taught in one burst. It is built layer by layer.

This is perhaps why her answer feels especially grounded. She is not speaking of AI as a theoretical disruption from the outside. She is looking at it through the lens of someone who has seen finance change already through technology, scale, globalization, and transformation.

AI, to her, is not a distant possibility. It is the next natural acceleration.

And like all accelerations, it will reward those who have range.

WHY AI ENTERS FINANCE SO EASILY

There are some professions where AI has to fight to find a foothold.

Finance is not one of them.

Finance is structured.

Finance is data-rich.

Finance is rule-based in many areas.

Finance depends heavily on repetition, consistency, classification, validation, and pattern recognition.

This makes it highly fertile ground for AI.

Tejaswini puts it plainly: finance has been transformed because finance is based on data. When the data is hygienic, much of the work that once required human effort - data crunching, data parsing, even deriving insights - can increasingly be handled by AI.

That phrase "hygienic data" is worth pausing over.

Because AI is only as useful as the quality of the data it works on. Dirty, fragmented, inconsistent data creates noise. But where data quality is strong, AI can do in seconds what once demanded teams, time, and repeated rounds of review.

And then there is accounting.

A large part of accounting is rule-based. There are principles, structures, classifications, treatments, workflows, checks, and recurring process logic. That makes it highly automatable over time.

For years, companies have already used systems to reduce manual accounting effort. AI takes that process further, not merely by recording and processing faster, but by recognizing patterns, flagging anomalies, and reducing the need for human intervention in large swathes of repetitive work.

This is where the future of finance starts becoming visible.

Not with the disappearance of finance itself.

But with the disappearance of finance work that is heavily mechanical.

And once the mechanical layer starts thinning out, the profession faces a deeper question:

What remains distinctively human?

"A large part of Finance is rule-based, such as Accounting, which can be done by AI."

THE ROLES THAT WILL FADE FIRST

Every time technology advances, we ask the same question.

What work is going away?

The answer is usually simpler than people expect. The first roles to shrink are the ones that depend least on human interpretation and most on repeated process execution.

Tejaswini identifies those roles as clerical in nature. The kind of work that is operationally necessary, but not strategically distinct.

One can imagine the category clearly.

Tasks built around repetitive preparation.

Tasks where the rules are fixed.

Tasks where output follows an expected pattern.

Tasks that require discipline, yes, but not much originality.

For years, finance teams had a large layer of such work. The function absorbed it because there was no alternative. If a report had to be prepared, it had to be prepared manually. If records had to be checked, someone had to check them. If data had to be processed, a human team processed it.

AI changes the economics of that equation.

Now the machine can perform a large share of those tasks more quickly, more consistently, and often with less fatigue-driven error than human teams.

That means the value attached to clerical finance work will decline.

Not because the work was unimportant.

But, because it is no longer a uniquely human contribution.

And once that happens, organizations begin to look elsewhere for value.

What they seek next, she says, are people who can envisage new ways of working within finance.

That is a striking phrase.

Not merely people who can "use AI."

Not merely people who are "digitally savvy."

But people who can rethink how finance itself should be organized and executed.

This is a higher-order skill.

It requires imagination, systems thinking, and comfort with change. It asks the finance professional not only to perform within a model, but to redesign the model.

That is where the next premium in finance talent may well lie.

THE DIFFERENCE IS NOT THE DEGREE. IT IS THE MINDSET

When I asked various finance leaders whether degrees matter more or skills, many tried to strike a balance.

Tejaswini does too, but then she goes one step further.

Degrees and skills, she says, are both valuable and both foundational. But what really differentiates top candidates is not degree or skill alone. It is mindset.

Curiosity.

Risk-taking.

Courage.

That is a remarkable answer from a CFO.

Because finance is often stereotyped as the last refuge of the cautious mind. Safe, measured, precise, conservative. The domain of people who like order more than adventure.

And yet, when one speaks to leaders who have risen to the top, a different picture emerges.

The best finance leaders are not reckless, but neither are they passive. They are often deeply curious. They are willing to look beyond the immediate task. They are willing to challenge assumptions. They are willing to rethink processes that others simply inherit. And they have the courage to engage with change rather than resist it.

That matters enormously in the AI era.

Because AI is not simply introducing a new tool, it is forcing a new way of thinking about work. The professionals who will benefit most from it are not necessarily the ones with the most polished résumé. They are the ones with the appetite to explore, adapt, and stretch.

Curiosity matters because the landscape is changing too quickly for static expertise to remain enough.

Risk-taking matters because every new tool, every new method, every redesigned workflow requires someone willing to try before the result is fully guaranteed.

Courage matters because professions do not transform politely. They unsettle identities. They threaten comfort. They expose complacency.

The people who thrive are not always the most decorated.

Sometimes, they are simply the least afraid of the future.

"Top candidates are differentiated not by skills and degrees... but by mindset, curiosity, risk-taking, and courage."

IS B.COM ENOUGH? HER ANSWER IS DIFFERENT

On the specific question of whether a B.Com degree is enough, her response is unusually brief.

Yes.

That may seem at odds with some of the other CFOs in this book, many of whom are more skeptical of a plain commerce degree as a sufficient marker in the modern market.

But her answer makes more sense when viewed alongside the larger point she is making. She is less interested in obsessing over credentials than in what happens after them.

For her, the bigger differentiator is not whether one started with a B.Com, but whether one remained intellectually alive after entering the profession.

This is where her emphasis on curiosity and courage returns.

A degree can still be enough to begin.

It is rarely enough to remain exceptional.

And perhaps that is the more useful interpretation.

Young professionals often worry too much about whether their first degree is perfect. In many cases, what matters more is how quickly they move from qualification to reinvention. A B.Com may give one the language of commerce and accounting, but in a world of AI, systems, automation, and changing business models, the real task begins after graduation.

How quickly do you evolve?

How willing are you to experiment?

How alert are you to what is happening in the world of technology and business?

How fast do you connect finance to the broader shifts in the world?

A foundational degree can still work.

A static mindset will not.

CAN AI TAKE OVER EVERYTHING? ALMOST

Some finance leaders draw firm boundaries around AI. "It will do this," they say, "but never that."

Tejaswini is more radical in her imagination.

AI can pretty much take over any task, she says.

That is a strong and somewhat unsettling proposition.

But she quickly follows it with the line that matters most: critical decision-making should always remain in human hands.

This is perhaps one of the clearest expressions of the tension we will see in the next decade.

At the level of capability, AI may continue expanding into more and more complex territory. Tasks once considered 'too judgment-heavy' may also become partially automatable. The system may draft analyses, propose responses, identify scenarios, recommend actions, and support decisions in ways that feel increasingly intelligent.

And yet, she insists, the final decision must still remain human.

Why?

Because there is a difference between being able to process a choice and being able to own a choice.

The first is computational.

The second is moral, managerial, and institutional.

A decision in finance often carries consequences far beyond the numbers. It affects trust, control, reputation, investor confidence, internal power, strategic direction, regulatory posture, human livelihood, and long-term resilience.

One may use AI to illuminate the choice.

One must not use AI to escape responsibility for the choice.

At least, not yet.

She adds that AI is not at a stage where it poses a holistic threat to the finance function. But she also leaves the door open: it will get there.

That is a realistic answer.

Too often, professionals comfort themselves with the idea that AI's limitations today will remain its limitations tomorrow. That is dangerous. The wiser approach is to recognize that capability will keep advancing, and therefore, one must keep redefining where human value truly lies.

Not in routine processing.

Not even in first-level analysis.

But in responsibility, discernment, and context-rich decision-making.

"AI can pretty much take over any task; however, critical decision-making should always be in human hands."

HUMANS AND ROBOTS, SIDE BY SIDE

When asked what finance teams will look like in the future, her answer reaches for a large historical analogy.

Humans and robots, she says, will be co-creating. It will be like the Industrial Revolution, where workers and machines coexist.

That is an evocative image.

The Industrial Revolution did not eliminate human work. It changed its character. It changed where value was created, which skills were prized, and how labor and machines related to one another.

Something similar may happen in finance.

The future finance team may not be split between 'finance people' and 'technology people' in the old sense. Instead, humans and intelligent systems may work in tandem, each doing what they are better suited to do.

The machine may process, classify, scan, flag, summarize, and predict.

The human may interpret, challenge, decide, communicate, and own.

This will not necessarily make finance easier. In some ways, it may make it more demanding.

Because once routine work is absorbed by machines, the average human contribution expected from finance professionals rises. The role becomes more strategic by force. One must be able to think more, not less.

At the same time, this coexistence can also be liberating.

Many finance professionals entered the field because they liked business thinking, structure, and commercial problem-solving, not because they dreamed of spending endless hours on repetitive process work. AI may finally allow the profession to spend more of its energy where its most capable people always wanted to contribute.

That, perhaps, is the optimistic reading.

Humans and machines will not simply coexist.

They may also free each other to do what they do best.

If that happens, the profession may become leaner, yes. But also more intellectually alive.

THE MOST IMPORTANT ADVICE SHE GIVES

Her final advice to young professionals is deceptively simple.

Be curious.

Stay on top of what is happening in the world of tech and the world.

It is an incredibly exciting time we live in.

There is a lot hidden inside that answer.

Firstly, she is telling finance aspirants not to become narrow. One cannot build a future-proof finance career by only reading accounting updates and tax amendments. Those matter, certainly. But the bigger shifts are often happening elsewhere - in technology, regulation, geopolitics, markets, data, business models, and societal change.

Finance leaders who understand only finance will increasingly feel blindsided. The profession is becoming more porous, more connected to everything else.

Second, she frames the present not as a time of fear, but as a time of possibility.

That matters.

Because every major transformation creates two emotional camps. One sees threat, the other sees excitement. Usually, the second group learns faster.

To be curious in such a world is not a personality trait alone. It is a career strategy.

Curiosity makes you explore before you are forced to.

It helps you understand tools before they become mandatory.

It allows you to connect dots that others notice too late.

It gives you energy in a period when many others only feel fatigue.

And perhaps that is the note on which this chapter lands best.

Not on fear of AI.

Not on mourning the decline of old roles.

But on the thrill of being alive in a profession that is being reinvented.

An exciting time, she says.

And if one listens carefully, that sounds less like a comment and more like an invitation.

WHAT TEJASWINI RAJWADE'S PERSPECTIVE REALLY SAYS ABOUT THE FUTURE

There is a particular honesty in the way Tejaswini sees the future.

She does not minimize AI's power.

She does not over-romanticize human exclusivity.

She does not cling to the safety of traditional finance work.

Instead, she accepts that AI may eventually take over far more than people currently imagine.

And then she asks the only useful question: where does human value remain?

Her answer is not technical. It is human.

In mindset.

In curiosity.

In courage.

In envisioning new ways of working.

In making critical decisions.

In owning consequences.

In staying open to a changing world.

This is an important contribution to the broader theme of this book.

Because the future of jobs in finance is not only about tasks and tools, it is about human posture.

Will finance professionals approach the future defensively, trying to preserve yesterday's comfort?

Or will they approach it creatively, asking how they can become larger than the work that is being automated?

Tejaswini Rajwade seems to belong firmly to the second camp.

And that is what makes her perspective worth listening to.

ADVICE TO YOUNG PROFESSIONALS

Be curious.

In times of rapid change, curiosity is not optional. It is an advantage.

Do not define yourself too narrowly.

The future of finance is being shaped by technology, business, and global change together.

Stay close to what is happening in the world.

Do not confine your learning to finance textbooks and internal processes.

Accept that repetitive work will decline.

Prepare yourself for roles that require judgment, redesign, and strategic thinking.

Learn to work with AI early.

Those who understand how to use it will have a much stronger edge.

Value mindset as much as credentials.

Degrees and skills matter, but mindset determines how far you will go.

Take risks.

Professionals who can envision new ways of working will be more valuable than those who only preserve the old.

Hold on to human judgment.

Even if AI becomes highly capable, critical decisions must still carry human ownership.

See this era for what it is.

Not just disruptive, but exciting.

Chapter 9

The Question Asker

ANKIT GHEEDIA, GROUP MANAGER, MICROSOFT

Some leaders describe the future in careful percentages.

A little automation here.

Some productivity improvement there.

A few roles redesigned.

A few workflows optimized.

Ankit Gheedia does not take that route.

His view is sharper, almost abrupt: the future of work will change fully. Nothing will remain as it is today.

It is a bold statement, but it captures something many professionals are sensing quietly. AI is not just another tool added to the workplace. It is changing the shape of work itself. The old assumption was that technology would improve existing jobs. The new possibility is more unsettling: technology may make us reimagine what those jobs are in the first place.

Ankit's own journey, as he describes it, has been one of continuous learning. Company shifts were turning points. AI is now another, not a small turning point, but a large one, the kind that changes how people think about careers, capability, and relevance.

He does not over-explain the past. His focus is clearly on what comes next.

And what comes next, in his view, is not a minor adjustment.

It is a complete reimagination.

"It will change fully. Nothing will remain as it is now."

WHEN CHANGE STOPS BEING INCREMENTAL

Most professionals are comfortable with incremental change.

A new software system.

A new process.

A new reporting line.

A new operating model.

A new tool that makes one part of the job faster.

Incremental change is manageable because it allows people to keep their old identity. You are still the same professional, doing mostly the same work, only with a better tool.

AI challenges that comfort.

Ankit's response suggests that we may be entering a phase where work is not simply improved, but redesigned. The question is not, 'How will AI help me do my current job better?' The deeper question is, 'Will my current job continue to exist in this form at all?'

That is a very different question.

In finance, accounting, audit, technology, operations, and almost every knowledge function, many tasks are already being broken down into smaller units that AI can support or execute. Once this happens at scale, organizations will no longer design roles around old task bundles. They will design them around outcomes.

That means job descriptions will change.

Team structures will change.

The meaning of productivity will change.

The value of human contribution will change.

This is what "fully changed" really means.

Not that every human disappears.

But that the old map of work becomes unreliable.

THE 90% POSSIBILITY

One of Ankit's strongest statements is that in the next ten to fifteen years, perhaps 90% of our activities will be automated.

That number is less important than the direction of thought behind it.

He is not saying 90% of people will disappear. He is saying 90% of activities may change hands. That distinction matters.

A job is not one thing. It is a bundle of activities. Some are repetitive, some are judgment-based, some involve coordination, some require communication, some need creativity, and some require asking the right question at the right time.

AI will attack the activity layer first.

Emails, summaries, follow-ups, first drafts, analysis, pattern recognition, workflow routing, data checks, report preparation, system updates, operational monitoring: all of these can be automated or heavily assisted.

When enough activities inside a role are automated, the role itself starts changing.

That is why Ankit says, maybe we will start doing something completely different.

It sounds extreme, but it is a practical possibility.

If 90% of what a person currently does can be automated, the organization will not ask that person to keep doing the remaining 10% in the old way. It will redesign the role around new value.

The future professional, then, cannot think only in terms of protecting tasks.

Tasks are fragile.

Capability is more durable.

The real question becomes: what can you do when the task is no longer the point?

"Ten to fifteen years is a huge timeline. Ninety percent of our activities may be automated."

THE ROLES THAT WILL BE REIMAGINED

Ankit does not list specific roles that will decline. Instead, he says the whole thing will be completely reimagined.

That answer is broad, but useful.

Because in some transformations, asking, "Which role will decline?" is too narrow. Roles do not always disappear cleanly. They mutate.

A business analyst may become an AI-enabled problem framer.

A finance analyst may become a decision partner.

An operations manager may become an automation orchestrator.

A team lead may become a human-machine workflow designer.

A technology manager may spend less time coordinating execution and more time shaping systems of intelligence.

The old role names may remain for some time, but the work underneath them will be different.

This is why young professionals should be careful about attaching their identity too strongly to a job title.

Titles lag reality.

The work changes first.

The title changes later.

By the time the title changes, the market has already moved.

Ankit's view pushes professionals to prepare for the underlying shift, not merely the visible one. If the workplace is being reimagined, then the safest career strategy is not to become excellent only at today's process. It is to become excellent at learning new processes, questioning assumptions, and adapting quickly.

That is where his list of future skills becomes important.

THE SKILLS THAT WILL MATTER

Ankit names four capabilities that will matter deeply:

Critical thinking.

Asking the right questions.

Agility.

Systems thinking.

This is a compact list, but it is highly relevant to an AI-led future.

Critical thinking matters because AI will produce answers quickly. But speed is not the same as correctness. Professionals will need to evaluate outputs, challenge assumptions, spot gaps, and understand when an answer looks good but rests on weak logic.

Asking the right questions may become even more valuable than knowing the right answers. In an AI environment, prompts, problem framing, and judgment around inquiry matter. The person who asks a shallow question will get a shallow answer faster. The person who asks a sharper question will create value.

Agility matters because tools, workflows, and expectations will keep changing. A slow learner will struggle. A rigid professional will struggle even more. Agility is not just speed. It is the ability to shift without losing effectiveness.

Systems thinking matters because AI does not operate in isolation. It changes workflows, dependencies, incentives, risks, and outcomes. A narrow professional may optimize one task and damage the larger system. A systems thinker understands how one change affects the whole.

Together, these capabilities point to a clear future profile.

The valuable professional will not merely execute.

The valuable professional will diagnose, question, connect, and adapt.

"Critical thinking, asking the right questions, agility, and systems thinking will matter."

DEGREES VERSUS LEARNING MINDSET

On the question of degrees, Ankit's answer is direct: learning on the go and a learning mindset will matter more than degrees.

This does not mean degrees have no value. It means degrees are no longer enough to define long-term professional relevance.

A degree captures what you learned at one point in time.

A learning mindset determines whether you remain useful as the world changes.

That distinction is becoming central to the future of work.

In earlier career models, formal education gave professionals a long runway. You studied, entered a field, accumulated experience, and progressed. The knowledge base changed, but not always at a pace that threatened your identity every few years.

AI compresses that cycle.

Tools change faster.

Methods change faster.

Expectations change faster.

Old competence becomes ordinary faster.

So, the professional who waits for formal training will always be late.

Learning on the go becomes essential, not as a motivational slogan, but as a survival skill.

This is especially true for students and young professionals. They should not ask only, "Which degree will make me safe?" They should ask, "How quickly can I learn what the market starts valuing next?"

Because safety will not come from one credential.

It will come from adaptability.

THE NEW PROFESSIONAL IDENTITY

If Ankit's view is taken seriously, then the future professional cannot be built around static expertise alone.

The future professional must be experimental.

Not careless.

Not random.

But experimental.

Experimenting means trying new tools before they become compulsory. It means using AI in small ways to understand its strengths and limits. It means testing workflows, learning from failure, and building comfort with uncertainty.

This is why his advice is simple: keep learning and experimenting.

There is no elaborate framework here. No long list of certifications. No complicated career formula.

Just two verbs.

Learn.

Experiment.

Those two verbs may be enough.

Because the next ten to fifteen years are too uncertain for rigid planning, if 90% of activities may be automated, then no one can confidently map every future job title. What one can build is the habit of staying current and the courage to try.

Experimentation also reduces fear.

The professional who has never used AI seriously will imagine it as either magic or threat. The professional who experiments with it daily will see it more accurately: useful, flawed, powerful, limited, and evolving.

That realistic familiarity will matter.

WHAT THIS MEANS FOR FINANCE AND BUSINESS ROLES

Although Ankit comes from the technology sector, his view applies strongly to finance and business careers.

Finance roles are activity-heavy.

So are audit, accounting, compliance, reporting, operations, and analysis roles.

If AI automates large portions of these activities, then the human premium shifts elsewhere:

- framing business problems
- asking better questions

- interpreting outputs
- connecting decisions across systems
- communicating implications
- challenging machine-generated conclusions
- redesigning workflows
- managing change

This is where systems thinking becomes especially important.

A finance professional who only understands a report may be replaced by a system that generates it. A finance professional who understands how the report affects decisions, incentives, risks, and business outcomes remains valuable.

The same logic applies in technology.

A manager who only tracks tasks may become less relevant. A manager who can design better ways for humans and AI systems to work together becomes more relevant.

The future, therefore, will not reward passive tool users.

It will reward people who can redesign work around tools.

THE REAL WARNING IN ANKIT'S RESPONSE

The most important thing about Ankit's response is not the exact prediction that 90% of activities may be automated.

The important thing is the urgency.

He is essentially saying: do not assume continuity.

Do not assume your current job will remain structurally similar.

Do not assume your degree will protect you.

Do not assume execution alone will be enough.

Do not assume change will arrive slowly enough for you to react later.

This is a useful warning.

Professionals often underestimate change because daily life still looks normal. The meetings continue. The dashboards continue. The reports continue. The job titles continue. But underneath, the economics of work may already be shifting.

AI does not need to replace a full role in one stroke. It only needs to keep removing activities from it.

At some point, the role has to be rebuilt.

That is the future Ankit is pointing toward.

ADVICE TO YOUNG PROFESSIONALS

Keep learning continuously.

Your degree may help you start, but your learning mindset will determine how long you stay relevant.

Experiment with AI early.

Do not wait for your company or college to formally teach you everything.

Develop critical thinking.

Fast answers are not always good answers. Learn to question outputs.

Ask better questions.

In an AI-led world, the quality of your question will shape the quality of your result.

Build agility.

Roles, tools, and workflows will change. Your ability to adapt will matter.

Learn systems thinking.

Understand how one change affects the whole business or workflow.

Do not over-attach yourself to current tasks.

Many activities may be automated. Build capability beyond task execution.

Stay comfortable with uncertainty.

Ten to fifteen years is a long horizon. The goal is not to predict everything, but to remain adaptable.

Focus on reinvention.

The future may not simply give you a better version of your current job. It may ask you to do something else entirely.

Keep learning and experimenting.

That is the simplest and most practical career strategy in an AI-shaped world.

Chapter 10

The Fifth Life

SHAILESH HARIBHAKTI, CHAIRMAN, SHAILESH HARIBHAKTI ASSOCIATES

Some people build one career and spend the rest of their working lives defending it.

Others seem to live many careers inside a single lifetime.

They move from one field to another, not because they are restless in a trivial sense, but because they keep sensing where the next frontier lies. They do not merely adjust to change. They place themselves inside it.

Shailesh Haribhakti is one such person.

When he describes his own professional journey, he does not list designations in the standard, neat corporate format.

He says something far more evocative.

He is living his fifth life.

Student.

Teacher at IIMA.

Chairman of the fifth largest accounting firm in India.

Sustainability professional.

And now, an AI-led consultant.

That phrase stayed with me.

Not because it sounds dramatic, though it certainly does. But, hidden inside it is a lesson about the future of work itself. In an age shaped by AI, perhaps the most valuable people will not be those who cling to one identity too tightly. They will be those who can reinvent themselves without losing their center.

Haribhakti's view of the future is at once bold and strangely calm.

He is not speaking of small changes at the edge of consulting or accounting. He sees AI pushing services toward a new level of productivity altogether. Hyper-productive services, delivered at a scale never seen before. In his view, most routine and repetitive task-oriented jobs will fade. What rises in their place will be research, discovery, and deeper value creation.

And yet, he is equally clear that some things do not move to machines.

Human touch.

Sensitivity.

Ethics.

Culture.

These, he says in effect, remain with us.

In a world rushing breathlessly toward automation, it is a useful reminder. The future may be AI-led. It will still need to be human-guided.

"Routine, repetitive, task-oriented jobs will vanish, and research and discovery-oriented jobs will grow."

A CAREER OF MANY LIVES

There are professionals who can explain their careers in one line.

"I was always in finance."

"I spent my life in consulting."

"I stayed in one industry and grew with it."

Haribhakti's journey resists that kind of reduction.

He has moved through five identities, each large enough to have been a full career on its own.

The student, learning and absorbing.

The teacher at IIMA, shaping minds.

The accounting leader, building and guiding one of India's major firms.

The sustainability professional, stepping into one of the defining issues of our times.

And now, the AI-led consultant, entering yet another frontier.

This is not a conventional career arc. It is closer to a sequence of rebirths.

And perhaps that is why his perspective on AI feels different from that of many others. He is not looking at it from inside one narrow professional trench. He is looking at it as someone who has repeatedly moved across knowledge domains and seen firsthand how professions evolve, mature, and get disrupted.

That gives him a larger horizon.

He understands, perhaps more intuitively than most, that the real issue is not whether one profession or one role will change. It is whether human beings can keep changing with the world around them.

A person who has lived many professional lives is better positioned to say this than one who has spent decades defending a single territory.

There is also something deeply contemporary about the way he names his lives. Not jobs. Not posts. Lives.

That is a subtle but powerful distinction.

A job is something you do.

A life is something you inhabit.

And if work is increasingly going to be reshaped by AI, then perhaps the professionals who survive best will be the ones who know how to inhabit new forms of work without nostalgia for the old ones.

WHAT AI REALLY CHANGES: SCALE

When many leaders talk about AI, they speak first of efficiency.

Haribhakti's phrase is more forceful.

Hyper-productive services on a larger scale than ever before.

That is not just efficiency. That is leverage.

It suggests that AI will not merely shave time off existing workflows. It will allow entire classes of professional services to be delivered at levels of productivity and scale previously unimaginable.

This is a profound shift.

For decades, professional services have been constrained by human bandwidth. Even in highly intellectual fields, growth depended on hiring more people, training more people, and managing more teams. The model scaled, but only up to a point. The ratio between people and output remained stubbornly linked.

AI begins to break that ratio.

Now, the same service engine can potentially produce much more with fewer repetitive steps and more automated support. Research can be accelerated. Summaries generated quickly. Comparative analysis done rapidly. Drafting sped up. Data organized at scale. Pattern recognition sharpened. Knowledge retrieval widened.

In other words, one does not simply get 'faster work.' One gets a different unit economics of thinking work.

And once that happens, the profession itself changes shape.

Clients expect faster delivery.

Firms expect more output per person.

Leaders must rethink what a team should look like.

And professionals can no longer define their value by effort alone.

This is one of the hardest psychological shifts for traditional knowledge professions.

For a long time, intellectual work carried prestige because it was difficult, time consuming, and human-intensive. AI does not eliminate the difficulty of thought, but it changes the cost and speed of many of the supporting layers around thought.

So the premium shifts.

Not to the person who works the longest.

But to the person who creates the highest value, once the repetitive effort is reduced.

This is exactly where Haribhakti's phrase of "hyper-productive services" becomes so useful. It captures the future not as automation replacing service, but as service being amplified into something much more powerful.

And amplification, unlike replacement, raises an uncomfortable question.

If your service can now be delivered at scale, what part of your role remains special?

"Hyper-productive services on a larger scale than ever before."

THE WORK THAT WILL DISAPPEAR FIRST

Haribhakti is clear about the first layer of jobs that will vanish.

Routine.

Repetitive.

Task-oriented.

This is now a familiar pattern across industries, but in consulting, advisory, and accounting-related services, it acquires a special significance. These professions have long had a hidden engine of repetitive work beneath their high-value facade.

Background research.

Compilation.

Formatting.

Document review.

Initial drafting.

Low-level process execution.

The kind of work often delegated to junior staff, not because it required little intelligence, but because it was labor-intensive and teachable.

AI goes straight after this layer.

And once that layer begins to disappear, the old apprenticeship model of many knowledge professions also begins to shift. In the past, professionals often learned by doing exactly such repetitive work. They spent years in the lower layers before earning the right to interpret, advise, or lead.

What happens if those lower layers are no longer as central?

This is one of the biggest unanswered questions for the future of professional services.

The work may vanish.

But the learning journey must somehow still be rebuilt.

And that is why Haribhakti's answer does not stop with job loss. He immediately points to the kind of work that will grow.

Research.

Discovery.

This is important.

If routine work disappears, the remaining work becomes more exploratory. Less about following a template, more about asking the next question. Less about producing a standard answer, more about seeking a new one.

This is where AI paradoxically raises the bar for human professionals.

Because once machines do the repetitive, humans must become more original.

WHAT WILL GROW: RESEARCH, DISCOVERY, AND THE HUMAN EDGE

Research and discovery-oriented jobs, Haribhakti says, will grow.

That is an unusually elegant way of putting it.

He does not say 'strategic jobs' or 'value-added jobs' or 'higher-order work', though all of those would have been acceptable phrases. He says research and discovery.

Research suggests disciplined inquiry.

Discovery suggests newness.

Together, they point to the future shape of serious professional work.

The professional of tomorrow may spend less time executing standardized workflows and more time:

- exploring new patterns
- testing assumptions

- discovering possibilities
- creating insight from complexity
- connecting seemingly unrelated domains
- framing the next question, not just the current answer

In an AI-driven world, this kind of work becomes more important because machines, however powerful, still operate within boundaries of pattern and prediction. Humans remain especially valuable in sensing what question has not yet been asked, what meaning is hidden in weak signals, what contradiction deserves attention, what emerging issue needs a name.

That is discovery.

And then there is the line Haribhakti adds, almost as a counterweight to all this futurism: human touch and sensitivity will always be critical.

This is not sentimentality. It is strategy.

Professional work is not only about information. It is also about relationships, trust, timing, understanding the emotional and cultural subtext inside institutions, knowing when to push and when to pause, reading resistance, and recognizing that an answer can be technically correct and still wrong for the moment.

AI can process data.

Sensitivity interprets people.

And in leadership, in consulting, in advisory, in judgment-heavy work, that difference will remain enormous.

The more technologically advanced the world becomes, the more visible this contrast may grow.

The machine can scale.

The human can sense.

"Human touch and sensitivity will always be critical."

THE MINDSET THAT WILL SURVIVE AI

Haribhakti's answer on skills is stripped down to the essentials.

Curiosity.

Persistence.

A continuous hunger to learn.

No long list of software tools.

No catalog of qualifications.

No inflated language.

Just three qualities.

And perhaps that is exactly right.

Because, in a world changing this fast, the specific tool may matter for a while. The deeper posture matters for much longer.

Curiosity matters because one cannot work well with the future if one does not remain interested in it. Curiosity is what prevents professionals from becoming defensive too early. It is what makes them ask, “What is this tool capable of?” instead of only, “Will this tool threaten me?”

Persistence matters because adaptation is usually awkward before it becomes rewarding. New systems frustrate, new methods fail, and reinvention is rarely graceful in the early stages. The person who keeps going through that discomfort gains an advantage over the one who gives up after the first confusion.

And a hunger to learn matters because no stable plateau of expertise exists anymore. The half-life of knowledge is shortening. The person who stops learning is not resting. They are declining.

These qualities sound almost timeless, and that is perhaps the deeper point.

Technology changes.

The human qualities that help one absorb change remain surprisingly constant.

That may be why Haribhakti, despite operating at the frontier of AI-led consulting, returns not to an app, a platform, or a technical framework, but to traits of mind.

The future may reward digital fluency.

It will still be entered through human curiosity.

ARE TRADITIONAL DEGREES ENOUGH? MAYBE, BUT NOT FOR LONG

His answer on traditional degrees is as intriguing as it is provocative.

Maybe, he says, for a few years. Until we have a polymathic, personal AI tutor for each human, downloadable from the internet for free.

That line opens an entirely different window into the future of education.

Most finance and consulting leaders answer this question in the present tense: what degrees are enough today, what professional qualifications matter, what certifications add value.

Haribhakti's answer jumps ahead.

He imagines a world where the monopoly of formal education over knowledge has broken down far more dramatically than it has so far. A world in which every person may have access to deeply capable personalized learning support at almost no cost.

If that happens, the meaning of "qualification" changes.

Not overnight.

Not completely.

But fundamentally.

Formal degrees may continue to matter as signals for some time. They structure early careers, provide social proof, and help employers filter candidates. But if high-quality learning becomes radically democratized through AI, then the premium shifts even more strongly toward what one can do with knowledge rather than where one acquired it.

This is a very different way of thinking about future careers.

It suggests that traditional degrees may retain temporary relevance, but not permanent supremacy. What will matter more over time is whether the individual keeps learning, updating, and integrating knowledge across disciplines.

And that links back to another phrase in his answer: polymathic.

The future, in his imagination, belongs not to the narrowly trained expert alone, but to the person who can think across fields. That is a strikingly old idea in a very new technological age.

The specialist may still survive.

The polymath may flourish.

"All aspects will be AI-led, but the orchestration of value will always need humans."

WHAT AI CAN LEAD, AND WHAT HUMANS MUST ORCHESTRATE

One of the strongest sentences in Haribhakti's response is also one of the shortest.

All aspects will be AI-led. But the orchestration of value will always need humans.

There is a lot compressed inside that line.

First, he is not underestimating AI. He is saying quite explicitly that AI will lead across aspects of work. This is not a timid or guarded view of technology. It is a recognition that AI will increasingly become central to execution, insight generation, and operating models.

But then comes the second half: orchestration of value.

That phrase is beautiful because it moves the conversation away from tasks and into architecture.

Orchestration means:

- deciding what matters
- aligning moving parts
- ensuring coherence
- making trade-offs
- governing outcomes
- creating value out of many coordinated elements

In a sense, AI may handle more and more pieces of the instrument panel. Humans still conduct the orchestra.

This is a particularly useful way to think about the future of professional work. Too often, people ask whether a task can be automated. The better question may be: who designs, directs, and takes responsibility for the value created by this automated system?

That is orchestration.

And then Haribhakti adds the final anchors: ethics and culture will always remain with humans.

Again, he is identifying the residue of humanity at the top of the machine stack.

A machine can optimize.

A culture tells you what is worth optimizing.

A machine can recommend.

Ethics tells you what should not be done, even if it can be done.

A machine can scale action.

Culture determines how that scale is experienced inside institutions and society.

This is why his final advice is so compressed and so serious: embrace AI ethics and values.

In a world infatuated with capability, he is reminding us to stay conscious of conscience.

That may be one of the most important themes in your entire book.

THE CONSULTANT OF THE FUTURE

If one tries to imagine the professional archetype emerging from Haribhakti's answers, it would look something like this:

A learner across domains.

A professional comfortable with AI-led work.

A person less attached to routine execution and more drawn to research, discovery, and synthesis.

Someone who can work with machines without surrendering judgment.

Someone who sees ethics and culture not as afterthoughts, but as central to value creation.

Someone who can orchestrate, not merely perform.

This is not just the future consultant.

It may be the future leader in any knowledge profession.

There is also something deeply hopeful in his perspective.

He does not describe AI as a shrinking force. He describes it as an enlarging one. A force that can make services hyper-productive, expand research, and create possibilities at scale. But only if humans rise to the task of guiding that power well.

That "if" matters.

Technology does not automatically improve human outcomes.

It magnifies the quality of the intentions and systems around it.

Which is why ethics and culture are not decorative add-ons.

They are control systems.

Without them, scale becomes dangerous.

With them, scale becomes valuable.

WHAT SHAILESH HARIBHAKTI'S VIEW REALLY MEANS

There are leaders who respond to AI with operational advice. Learn this tool. Use that system. Automate this process.

Haribhakti's response operates at a different altitude.

He is really asking a larger question: what kind of human being should one become in a world where AI enters every layer of work?

His answer is not fear.

It is reinvention.

Not nostalgia.

But range.

Not defensive expertise.

But polymathic curiosity.

Not rigid profession.

But many lives.

That, perhaps, is why this chapter belongs in a book about the future of jobs in finance and adjacent fields. Because the deepest disruption may not be about jobs at all. It may be about identity.

Will we cling to the first version of ourselves?

Or will we have the courage to live a second, third, fourth, even fifth professional life?

Haribhakti seems to suggest that the latter is not only possible, it may become necessary.

And if so, the future belongs not to the most settled.

But to the most alive.

ADVICE TO YOUNG PROFESSIONALS

Cultivate curiosity.

The future belongs to people who remain genuinely interested in what is changing.

Persist through discomfort.

Every major shift feels awkward at first. Keep going.

Stay hungry to learn.

A static professional is a declining professional in the AI era.

Do not over-attach yourself to routine work.

The repetitive layers of professional services are the first to be automated.

Move toward research and discovery.

That is where human contribution will deepen.

Learn to work with AI, not around it.

The professions of the future will be AI-led in many aspects.

Hold on to human touch and sensitivity.

These will remain critical, even in highly automated environments.

Think in terms of value orchestration.

It will matter less that you "did the task" and more that you shaped meaningful outcomes.

Take ethics seriously.

In the age of intelligent systems, values become more important, not less.

Build a life, not just a designation.

The future may ask you to reinvent yourself more than once.

Chapter 11

The Value Architect

ABHISHEK GUPTA, CFO, LIVSPACE

There was a time when the finance function was expected to do three things well.

Close the books.

Protect the controls.

Explain the variance.

If it did those three things with discipline and credibility, it was considered a strong function.

That time is ending.

Not because those responsibilities have disappeared. They have not. But because they are no longer enough. Artificial intelligence is changing the economics of finance work so deeply that the function itself is being pushed into a new identity. The old finance team processed and protected information. The new one will increasingly interpret, govern, and direct it.

Abhishek Gupta has seen enough versions of finance to know the difference.

His career has not been a sequence of random promotions. It has been a deliberate build. Every role, by his own account, added a different dimension to leadership. He began in audit, moved into commercial finance, then into global controls, sales finance, supply chain finance, category finance, wholesale finance, and eventually the CFO's chair in one of Indian e-commerce's most visible turnarounds.

Discipline.

Scale.

Controls.

Strategy.

Transformation.

That is the progression.

Which is why his view of AI is not superficial. He is not dazzled by the headline version of AI, the one that promises universal transformation in six months. Nor is he dismissive. He is precise. In his view, AI is not just automating finance. It is reimagining what finance teams do, how they think, and the value they create.

That is the right place to begin.

Because the future of jobs in finance is not about whether the spreadsheet survives. It will. The real question is whether the person using that spreadsheet still defines their worth by producing it.

Gupta's answer is clear.

If a task can be described as a set of rules applied to data, AI will eventually do it better.

That changes everything.

"AI is not just automating finance – it is fundamentally reimagining what finance teams do, how they think, and the value they create."

FROM DISCIPLINE TO TRANSFORMATION

Some finance leaders rise through technical mastery. Others rise through breadth. Abhishek Gupta's career seems to have drawn strength from both.

He started at ITC Limited in Corporate Internal Audit and then moved into Commercial Finance for the Lifestyle Division. Those are not glamorous starting points in the modern LinkedIn sense, but they are exactly the kind of foundations that produce serious finance leaders. Audit teaches rigor, control, skepticism, and respect for systems. Commercial finance teaches how businesses actually make money, how pricing, margin, distribution, and operating decisions translate into financial outcomes.

That early combination mattered.

It gave him the discipline of finance before the excitement of transformation. It taught him that value is not just created by growth. It is also protected by control.

Then came Hindustan Unilever, and with it, three roles that expanded the frame.

The first was in a technology-driven controls service center that applied technology to strengthen financial controls in 180 countries. That detail deserves attention. Long before AI became fashionable boardroom vocabulary, some parts of finance were already experimenting with intelligent automation, system-driven control frameworks, and global standardization. For Gupta, this was not theory. It was operating reality. He saw, early, what happens when finance scales through technology rather than only through headcount.

Then came Sales Finance, including the setting up of a standalone branch office in Lucknow from scratch. Few experiences sharpen a finance leader like building from zero in the field. One learns very quickly that business is not a spreadsheet abstraction. It is people, trade-offs, cash cycles, incentives, execution, and judgment. Later, as National Sales Finance Manager across three of HUL's five branches, he built what he calls commercial instinct at scale.

Then came Supply Chain Finance for Personal Care across South Asia, a role that sits at the intersection of operational complexity and financial strategy. By that point, the finance lens had widened from control to commerce to operations.

Then came Flipkart.

At Flipkart, Gupta headed Category Finance for Private Brands, Electronics, and Furniture, some of the most strategically important and capital-intensive categories in Indian e-commerce. He also handled B2B Wholesale Finance. This gave him exposure not only to online retail economics but to portfolio decisions, inventory intensity, category-level profitability, vendor dynamics, and channel finance.

By the time he reached Myntra as CFO, the base was ready.

And it is there, by his own description, that the defining chapter of his career was written.

At Myntra, he led one of Indian e-commerce's most notable profitability turnarounds while simultaneously delivering growth and market share gains. That combination is rare enough in business to earn its own respect. Growth often comes at the cost of profitability. Profitability often comes through growth sacrifice. Market share is often bought with margin. To hold all three together is unusual. He describes it, correctly, as a trifecta.

It also earned him the CFO of the Year award in Digital and E-Commerce from CII and ASSOCHAM.

But the more important point is this: each transition in his career was deliberate. From discipline to scale. From controls to strategy. From management to transformation.

That sequence now shapes the way he sees the future of finance.

THE FIRST PLACE AI CHANGED FINANCE: CONTROLS

Many people think AI entered finance through analytics dashboards, forecasting tools, or chatbot assistants.

Gupta's lived experience points to something deeper.

He had already worked in an environment where technology was used to standardize and strengthen controls across 180 countries. In other words, finance had begun its machine-assisted future in the domain of reliability long before the current wave of AI hype.

That matters because controls are the skeleton of finance. If you can strengthen controls through system intelligence, you change not only efficiency but trust.

And today, AI has taken that further.

Gupta describes a world where anomaly detection, real-time transaction monitoring, and predictive risk flagging are changing internal audit from a periodic, backward-looking function into a continuous, forward-looking intelligence layer.

This is not just a faster audit. It is a different kind of audit.

The old audit came in cycles. It sampled, reviewed, and reported after the fact.

The new audit, or at least the version AI makes possible, lives closer to the flow of business. It senses. It flags. It monitors. It can act as an intelligence layer rather than a compliance ritual.

That is a profound shift.

Because the value of finance rises sharply when insight arrives, while corrective action is still possible.

The auditor, in Gupta's framing, moves from examiner to risk architect.

That phrase captures the future of many finance roles, not just audit. AI is not removing the function. It is pushing the human deeper into design, interpretation, and oversight.

"The auditor's role is shifting from examiner to risk architect."

ACCOUNTING: THE HYPE, THE HOPE, AND THE HONEST TRUTH

It is easy to make dramatic claims about AI in accounting. Gupta does not.

His answer here is one of the most nuanced and credible in the entire set of interviews.

He acknowledges that accounting is where some of the most grounded and consequential AI transformation is taking place. Repetitive journal entries, three-way reconciliations, invoice processing, intercompany matching: in organizations with the right data infrastructure, real efficiency gains are already visible. Month-end close timelines are compressing in pockets. Exception-based workflows are reducing manual effort.

But he is equally clear that the dream of a fully AI-driven, continuous-close accounting function remains aspirational for most organizations.

Why?

Because the barriers are real.

Fragmented ERP landscapes.

Poor data quality.

Regulatory conservatism around automated entries.

The deeply judgment-intensive nature of provisioning, revenue recognition, and audit trails.

That list matters because it grounds the conversation. AI can automate where the structure is strong. It struggles where environments are fragmented, standards are sensitive, and judgment is embedded in the process itself.

So, where is AI genuinely adding value today in accounting?

Flagging unusual accrual patterns.

Assisting reconciliations at scale.

Extracting structured data from unstructured documents, such as contracts and invoices.

These are real productivity gains. But, in his words, they are not yet full transformation.

That distinction is important for young professionals. One can respect AI's growing power without pretending every finance process will be re-engineered instantly. The smart finance leader prepares for gradual but relentless change, not magical overnight reinvention.

Gupta's broader conclusion is that the accountant's role is evolving gradually rather than dramatically. It is shifting toward exception management and financial judgment, while automation handles the high-volume, low-complexity work.

That is exactly the kind of clear-eyed realism the profession needs.

WHEN THE CFO LEADS AI, IT STOPS BEING AN IT PROJECT

One of the strongest insights in Gupta's chapter comes from Myntra.

He describes AI-driven fraud detection models that materially reduced payment fraud losses while protecting customer experience. He also describes intelligent payment routing that improved success rates and reduced transaction costs at scale.

He is careful to make a point that many organizations still miss.

These were not IT projects.

They were CFO-led, P&L-impacting initiatives.

That distinction is critical.

A technology initiative becomes strategically meaningful only when it solves a business problem that matters to the economics of the enterprise. A CFO who understands this does not merely sponsor automation. He or she allocates it against value pools.

Fraud reduction affects losses.

Payment optimization affects conversion and cost.

Both affect profitability.

That is finance-led AI.

Not a pilot for presentation slides.

A business lever.

WORKING CAPITAL CHANGES WHEN FORECASTS GET SMARTER

AI's impact is often discussed in abstract terms. Gupta brings it back to the bloodstream of business.

Demand forecasting, he says, changed how they thought about inventory financing, vendor payments, and working capital cycles. When forecast accuracy improves, the entire cash conversion cycle tightens.

This is a deceptively simple insight.

Forecasting is not just about better planning decks. It affects real capital. If inventory is funded more intelligently, cash is freed up. If vendor cycles are aligned with better demand visibility, working capital pressure reduces. If finance teams are not spending weeks building bottom-up forecasts manually, they can spend more time interpreting what the signals actually mean.

This is where AI stops being about efficiency alone and becomes about enterprise quality.

Better signals create better decisions.

Better decisions create better economics.

That is why the future finance professional must know not only how to operate the model, but when to trust it, when to challenge it, and how to explain its implications to the business.

THE INVISIBLE REVOLUTION: SKU-LEVEL INTELLIGENCE

One of the less glamorous, but more powerful applications of AI that Gupta mentions is catalog and commercial finance intelligence.

At Myntra, AI-led catalog management supported pricing intelligence, markdown optimization, and contribution margin analysis at the SKU level. That gave commercial finance teams real-time profitability visibility that had previously been impossible at scale.

This is where AI alters the texture of decision-making.

In old retail models, one often managed through broad averages and post-facto review. But when margin, pricing, and inventory performance can be understood at the smallest useful commercial unit, the entire quality of the finance partnership changes.

Commercial finance becomes more granular.

More immediate.

More embedded.

More commercially muscular.

And that is the broader theme of Gupta's view of finance.

Finance is not shrinking.

It is getting closer to the business.

"The finance profession is not declining – it is upgrading."

THE JOBS THAT WILL DECLINE

Gupta is unambiguous about the first layer of finance work under pressure.

Accounts payable and receivable clerks.

Routine reconciliation analysts.

Transactional bookkeeping.

Management reporting roles are built around assembling and formatting data.

Compliance roles built around checking large transaction volumes.

All these are vulnerable because their primary output is assembly, verification, routine processing, or standard report preparation.

If AI can generate a first-cut MIS pack overnight, the analyst, whose main contribution was aggregation, loses relevance quickly. If continuous monitoring can identify anomalies without rest, large parts of transaction-checking work become less human-intensive.

The important word here is not 'immediately'. It is 'inevitably'.

Some of these roles may persist for a while because systems, data environments, and organizational habits take time to change. But the direction is one-way.

The machine is better at repetitive, rule-based, high-volume work.

The profession must move its people to where the machine is not enough.

THE JOBS THAT BECOME MORE IMPORTANT

What replaces the old finance work?

Gupta's answer is crisp.

Finance business partners.

FP&A professionals with AI fluency.

Risk, governance, and AI oversight roles.

Treasury and capital allocation strategists.

This is a very strong map of the future.

Finance business partners are future-proof because they sit in the zone of interpretation and strategic challenge. They do not merely report to the business. They think with the business.

FP&A professionals with AI fluency matter because forecasting will not disappear. It will become model-assisted. The skill then is not to build every number by hand, but to know when to trust the model, when to override it, and how to explain variance to non-technical stakeholders.

Risk, governance, and AI oversight roles rise because someone must ensure model integrity, validate assumptions, and make sure AI-enabled finance remains compliant and trustworthy.

Treasury, capital allocation, investor relations, and M&A remain deeply human because they are not merely analytical problems. They are judgment problems, conviction problems, and narrative problems.

Machines can inform these decisions.

They cannot own them.

Gupta then identifies the three defining skills of the next generation:

- data literacy
- financial storytelling
- adaptability

That is as concise a future-of-finance summary as one could want.

"Credentials get you considered. Character and capability get you chosen."

DEGREES OPEN THE DOOR. TRAJECTORY COMES FROM LAYERING

Gupta's answer on degrees is one of the strongest in the book.

A B.Com, he says, is a solid foundation. But it is rarely sufficient on its own to build a compelling finance career.

That is exactly right.

A degree gives one the language of finance. It helps build accounting literacy, economic basics, and structured entry into the profession. But modern finance requires more:

- analytical depth
- business context
- technology fluency
- communication capability
- strategic judgment

That is why he sees B.Com as a launchpad, not a destination.

The professionals who go far, in his experience, almost always layer the base degree with something more:

- CA, for technical controllership credibility
- CFA for investments and capital markets
- CMA or ACCA, depending on the path
- an MBA for strategic thinking and cross-functional breadth
- data and analytics learning for future readiness

His phrase "intentional layering" is useful.

That is the right way to think about finance education now.

The degree gives you entry.

The combination gives you a trajectory.

And the combination is not just academic. It includes technology, communication, and practical business exposure.

This is why Gupta says the candidates who rise fastest are not necessarily the ones with the most impressive degrees. They are the ones who combine technical fluency with business acumen and human judgment.

WHAT AI WILL TAKE OVER, AND WHAT IT WILL NEVER OWN

Gupta draws the line well.

AI will absorb the tasks that are repetitive, rule-based, and data-intensive.

- transaction processing
- journal entries
- reconciliations
- invoice matching
- expense categorization
- month-end reporting
- variance analysis templates
- standard MIS generation

- fraud pattern detection
- payment routing
- audit sampling
- tax computation
- demand forecasting
- cash flow modeling
- scenario planning at scale

The logic is simple. If a task can be described as a set of rules applied to data, AI will eventually do it better.

But then comes the boundary.

Strategic capital allocation.

Stakeholder and investor communication.

Crisis navigation.

Ethical judgment and governance.

Organizational leadership.

These remain human because they require context, trust, conviction, nerve, and moral weight.

A board wants to read the numbers, yes. But it also wants to look the CFO in the eye. Investors want analysis, yes. But they also want to assess belief. During a crisis, no one asks the model to hold the institution together. They ask leaders.

That is why Gupta's core conclusion is so important:

AI will take over tasks. It will not take over judgment.

The professionals who survive and thrive will be those who migrate their value consciously, early, and deliberately from task execution to judgment, influence, and leadership.

Not after the transition happens to them.

Before it does.

"AI will take over tasks. It will not take over judgment."

THE FINANCE TEAM OF 2035

Gupta offers one of the most vivid descriptions of the future finance team in this entire project.

The finance function of 2035–2040, he says, will be smaller in headcount, broader in mandate, and more strategically consequential than anything we recognize today.

That sentence deserves to be read twice.

Smaller in headcount because the transactional core of finance will shrink.

Broader in mandate because finance will no longer merely report and control; it will operate as a distributed intelligence layer across the organization.

More strategically consequential because the quality of finance insight, governance, and decision support will matter more as AI makes information abundant.

He sees finance business partners embedded alongside product, supply chain, and commercial teams, rather than sitting in centralized back-office structures. The monthly MIS pack, he says, will feel as antiquated as a fax machine.

That is a memorable image because it is true.

The old rhythm of finance was periodic.

The new rhythm will be live.

Shared service centers themselves will change. They will evolve from human-operated processing hubs into AI-orchestrated engines, with humans supervising exceptions, governance, and continuous improvement rather than doing the processing.

His estimate is stark: the finance team of 2035 may be one-third the size of today's equivalent, while operating at three times the analytical depth and business impact.

That is not a small change. It is a redesign of the function.

THE CFO OF 2035: CHIEF VALUE ARCHITECT

If the team changes that dramatically, what happens to the CFO?

Gupta's answer here is exceptional. He says the CFO is moving from scorekeeper to Chief Value Architect.

That phrase captures the future role beautifully.

The traditional pillars of reporting, controls, treasury, and compliance will remain. But as intelligent systems increasingly run those pillars with less manual intervention, the CFO's attention will move almost entirely toward forward-looking, judgment-intensive leadership.

He sees the CFO of 2035 as simultaneously:

- a strategic co-pilot to the CEO
- a technology governor
- a capital storyteller
- a talent architect
- a risk philosopher

Each of those phrases is worth unpacking.

Strategic co-pilot: the CFO owns not only financial outcomes, but the analytical and intelligence infrastructure that drives enterprise decisions.

Technology governor: AI systems influencing finance and the wider business require integrity, ethics, and governance. The CFO will be one of the natural owners of that discipline.

Capital storyteller: In a world of abundant data, the ability to craft a clear, credible narrative around performance, risk, and value creation becomes one of the most human and most important CFO skills.

Talent architect: Future finance teams must blend finance depth with data science, technology, and partnership capability. Building that mix becomes a core leadership job.

Risk philosopher: When businesses operate in volatile and uncertain environments, the CFO becomes an anchor for long-term thinking, resilience, and scenario design.

And yet, Gupta is equally clear that some things will not change.

Integrity in reporting.

Stewardship.

The courage to speak truth to power.

The wisdom to navigate ethical complexity.

The responsibility to develop the next generation.

That is the continuity beneath the transformation.

The tools change.

The stewardship remains.

THE ADVICE THAT COMES FROM A FULL JOURNEY

Gupta's advice to young professionals is not formulaic. It has the tone of someone who has made choices, taken detours, made mistakes, and built perspective over time.

Master the fundamentals deeply.

Seek breadth early and depth later.

Become comfortable with technology now.

Invest in communication as seriously as technical skill.

Build your ethical compass early.

Find mentors, not just managers.

Stay curious and stay humble.

Find your purpose in the work.

There is a great deal of truth in his suggestion that early-career professionals should optimize for exposure over compensation. Controllership, commercial finance, FP&A, and business partnering all give different lenses. The people who become great CFOs are rarely those who spent their entire early career in one narrow box.

His warning about integrity is also worth underlining. Finance sits at the intersection of performance and truth. The moments that define reputation come earlier than most people expect, and in smaller ways than they imagine.

Guarding that ethical spine is not optional. It is the profession.

And his final thought may be the most elegant of all: finance, at its best, is not about numbers alone. It is about enabling growth, protecting stakeholders, allocating capital wisely, and creating sustainable value.

That is why, in his view, the world does not need more finance professionals who are merely good with numbers.

It needs finance leaders who are wise with judgment, brave with integrity, and generous with their knowledge.

ADVICE TO YOUNG PROFESSIONALS

Master the fundamentals deeply.

Know how the P&L, balance sheet, and cash flow connect. No technology fluency can compensate for weak financial basics.

Seek breadth early.

Work across controllership, commercial finance, FP&A, and business partnering, if possible. Exposure compounds.

Optimize for learning, not just salary.

Early-career breadth matters more than short-term compensation.

Build AI and technology fluency now.

You do not need to become a data scientist, but you must become a confident and curious user of technology.

Learn to work with AI outputs.

The future professional will need to question assumptions, interpret model output, and use tools intelligently.

Invest in communication.

The ability to convert complex financial reality into a clear narrative is a major career advantage.

Protect your integrity.

Your reputation in finance is built in moments when you are tempted to stay silent, soften the truth, or compromise.

Find mentors.

The right mentor can compress years of learning into months.

Stay curious and humble.

The finance function is changing fast. Defensiveness will age you quickly; curiosity will keep you relevant.

Remember the larger purpose.

Finance is not just a profession of numbers. It is a profession of stewardship, judgment, and value creation.

Conclusion

The Work That Remains

At the beginning of this book, the question seemed simple.

What will AI do to jobs in finance?

By the end of these conversations, it became clear that this was not the most useful question.

The better question is this:

What kind of finance work remains valuable when the machine can already do so much of what the profession once called work?

That is the real subject of this book.

Not whether finance will survive.

It will.

Not whether AI will enter the function.

It already has.

Not whether some roles will disappear.

They will.

The deeper issue is whether finance professionals, finance teams, and finance leaders can move their value fast enough from execution to judgment, from process to insight, from reporting to decision-making, and from functional excellence to enterprise influence.

That is the transition now underway.

And once one sees it clearly, the future of jobs in finance stops looking like a story of decline.

It starts looking like a story of redesign.

THE FUNCTION IS NOT SHRINKING. IT IS MOVING

One of the strongest ideas to emerge from these leaders is that finance is not becoming less important. If anything, it is becoming more consequential.

But it is also becoming less forgiving.

For years, the profession could absorb large layers of repetitive work because someone had to do them. Transactions had to be processed. Reports had to be assembled. Reconciliations had to be checked. Variances had to be compiled. Audit samples had to be reviewed. Data had to be gathered before anyone could discuss what it meant.

That old model created careers.

It also created comfort.

One could build a long and respectable future in finance by being dependable inside structure, by mastering the process, by producing accurate work, and by earning trust through discipline.

None of that becomes unimportant.

But much of it becomes insufficient.

Because if a task can be described as repetitive, rule-based, and data-intensive, AI will increasingly do it faster, cheaper, and often more accurately. That is true in accounting, audit, reporting, treasury support, compliance, forecasting support, controls, shared services, commercial analysis, tax, and consulting.

The pattern is now visible across the entire finance landscape.

The routine layer thins.

The judgment layer rises.

The human premium shifts upward.

That is why so many of the leaders in this book did not describe finance as dying. They described it as restructuring, upgrading, reimagining, or even becoming unrecognizable in its old form.

Those are strong words. But they are defensible.

The monthly MIS pack will not vanish because reporting vanishes. It will vanish because static reporting is no longer enough. Periodic controls will not vanish because risk disappears. They will vanish because continuous monitoring becomes possible. Transaction-heavy teams will not vanish because the business stops needing records. They will shrink because the system can increasingly create, validate, route, and analyze those records on its own.

The function remains.

The center of gravity moves.

THE CAREER LADDER IS CHANGING FASTER THAN MANY PEOPLE REALIZE

This matters most, perhaps, for the people entering finance now.

For decades, the profession had a fairly recognizable career ladder. One started with fundamentals, entered through a technical role, learned through repetition, moved into review, then into analysis, then into leadership.

That ladder is still standing, but some of its lowest steps are weakening.

If entry-level work is increasingly automated, then young professionals can no longer assume that time spent in routine execution will naturally turn into future relevance. They must become larger than repetitive work earlier.

This is why the leaders in this book kept returning to the same themes.

Degrees still matter.

But degrees alone are not enough.

A B.Com may still give language. A CA, CPA, CMA, ACCA, or CFA may still give technical credibility. An MBA may still widen business perspective. These remain useful foundations.

But the foundation is not differentiation.

The differentiator now lies in what one layers on top:

- data literacy
- technology fluency
- AI awareness

- communication skill
- business context
- professional skepticism
- adaptability
- learning agility

This is not just a longer shopping list of modern skills. It reflects a structural truth.

The future finance professional cannot live in one narrow silo for too long.

The accountant who ignores technology will fade.

The analyst who cannot explain a business implication will plateau.

The manager, who only coordinates manual work, will become less relevant.

The finance professional who treats AI as someone else's problem will be overtaken by those who use it fluently.

What rises in place of the old narrow roles is a more hybrid professional identity.

The finance business partner.

The AI-enabled analyst.

The continuous auditor.

The techno-functional finance engineer.

The risk architect.

The capital storyteller.

The human who can still ask the better question after the machine has supplied the faster answer.

That is the new career terrain.

It is more demanding.

It is also more interesting.

THE NEW PREMIUM IS NOT INFORMATION. IT IS INTERPRETATION.

This may be the single most important shift in the whole book.

For a long time, finance professionals created value partly because information was difficult to collect, clean, structure, and present. The effort involved in producing a reliable financial view was itself a source of professional importance.

AI changes that.

When information becomes easier to retrieve, summarize, compare, and model, the value of access declines. The value of interpretation rises.

That sounds simple. It is not.

Because interpretation is harder to fake.

Anyone can produce a report.

Far fewer can explain what it means.

Fewer still can explain what should be done about it.

And fewer still can do so with clarity, conviction, and sound judgment when the situation is ambiguous.

This is why the future of finance will reward people who can move beyond the mechanics of numbers into the meaning of numbers.

What risk do they signal?

What assumption do they hide?

What trade-off do they expose?

What decision do they force?

What story do they tell about the health of the business?

What future do they imply if nothing changes?

These are not spreadsheet questions.

They are leadership questions.

And as AI becomes better at producing the first draft of the analysis, the premium on the final human reading of that analysis becomes even higher.

The machine may generate the output.

The professional still owns the conclusion.

THE CFO WILL NOT DISAPPEAR. THE CFO WILL EXPAND

If finance teams are changing this deeply, then the CFO role cannot remain untouched.

In fact, the opposite seems true.

The more AI takes over recurring work, the more the CFO moves toward the most human parts of enterprise leadership.

That is why, across these conversations, the CFO was described in ways that would have sounded unusual a decade ago.

Not merely the head of finance.

But the steward of value.

The trusted advisor.

The chief value architect.

The technology governor.

The capital storyteller.

The risk philosopher.

These are not decorative labels.

They reflect a real shift in expectation.

The old pillars of the job remain: reporting, controls, treasury, compliance, and capital discipline. But intelligent systems will increasingly run large parts of those pillars with less manual intervention than before. That frees the CFO's attention, but it also raises the standard.

The CFO of the future will be expected to:

- guide resource allocation with sharper judgment
- govern AI systems that influence financial outcomes
- ensure integrity survives automation
- help the CEO make better and faster decisions
- explain value creation credibly to boards, investors, and regulators

- build teams that combine finance depth with technology fluency
- hold steady in crisis when data is incomplete, and consequences are real

In other words, the CFO becomes less of a scorekeeper and more of an enterprise navigator.

This is not a smaller role.

It is a larger one, with fewer excuses.

Because once recurring process work becomes less visible, the truly human responsibilities of the CFO become more exposed:

judgment, courage, credibility, and stewardship.

That is why AI will not diminish the best finance leaders.

It will reveal them.

THE PART THAT DOES NOT AUTOMATE

There is a temptation, when discussing AI, to make everything sound replaceable until proven otherwise.

But these leaders returned, again and again, to the same boundary.

AI can automate tasks.

It cannot own judgment.

It can detect patterns.

It cannot carry moral responsibility.

It can optimize a workflow.

It cannot decide what ought to be optimized in the first place.

It can draft investor commentary.

It cannot replace trust between people.

It can support capital decisions.

It cannot carry the conviction of those decisions when they must be defended publicly.

It can analyze scenarios.

It cannot hold nerve in a crisis.

That is why the parts of finance that remain most valuable are also the parts that remain most human:

- ethical judgment
- professional skepticism
- stakeholder trust
- strategic conviction
- contextual reasoning
- talent development
- cultural leadership
- the courage to speak truth when the room would prefer comfort

This is not a sentimental defense of humanity. It is an operating fact.

The closer a decision comes to ambiguity, consequence, reputation, governance, or long-term value, the more human quality matters.

And finance lives very close to those decisions.

Which means the future of finance will not be less human.

It will be more demanding of human quality at a higher level.

WHAT THIS BOOK ULTIMATELY SAYS

If one had to reduce all these interviews to a single conclusion, it might be this:

The future belongs to finance professionals who consciously migrate their value before the market forces them to.

Not after their role becomes obsolete.

Before it does.

That migration has already started.

From bookkeeping to business partnership.

From controls execution to risk architecture.

From report preparation to decision support.

From transaction processing to exception governance.

From technical expertise alone to hybrid capability.

From title-based credibility to capability-based relevance.

This does not mean everyone must become a coder. It does not mean every finance professional must turn into a data scientist. It does not mean that old technical disciplines no longer matter.

It means the best finance careers of the next twenty years will be built by people who can combine:

- technical strength
- business understanding
- digital fluency
- communication ability
- learning agility
- ethical steadiness

That combination is difficult.

That is exactly why it will be valuable.

TO THE STUDENT, THE PROFESSIONAL, AND THE LEADER

If you are a student reading this, do not ask only which degree will get you a job. Ask what kind of capability stack will keep you useful when the job changes shape.

If you are an early-career professional, do not define your identity too tightly around the current task. Learn the fundamentals deeply, but move steadily toward interpretation, technology fluency, communication, and judgment.

If you are already in leadership, do not mistake current headcount and current process for future design. The function you manage today may not be the function you need tomorrow. Build for that truth early.

And if you are a CFO, the challenge is even sharper.

The future of the finance function will not be determined only by technology vendors, consultants, or AI systems. It will be determined by whether finance leaders choose to redesign their teams, upgrade their talent, govern automation wisely, and preserve the profession's ethical spine while its operating model changes.

That is the real leadership test of this era.

THE LAST WORD

Finance has always claimed to be the conscience of the business.

That claim is about to be tested.

In a world where machines can process, predict, reconcile, flag, route, and report at extraordinary speed, the profession will no longer be able to define itself by effort alone. It will have to define itself by judgment, by stewardship, by clarity, by trust, by the quality of the decisions it shapes and the standards it refuses to compromise.

That is a harder profession.

It is also a better one.

The old finance career rewarded those who could master the process.

The next one will reward those who can master meaning.

The old finance function reported what had happened.

The next one will increasingly help determine what happens next.

And the people who will matter most in that world will not be the ones who tried hardest to preserve yesterday's work.

They will be the ones who understood, early enough, what work was worth becoming.

About the Author

Sripal Jain is a Chartered Accountant, licensed US CPA, entrepreneur, educator, and Co-founder of Simandhar Education, one of India's leading institutions for US CPA, US CMA, EA, CIA, and other global accounting and finance qualifications.

He is the only Indian professional to be recognized consecutively among CPA Practice Advisor's 40 Under 40 Accounting Professionals and 20 Under 40 Accounting Influencers in the United States, a distinction awarded to emerging leaders shaping the future of the accounting profession.

Sripal has also been recognized among BW Education's 40 Under 40 Education Leaders and has received several accolades for his contributions to education, entrepreneurship, and the accounting profession.

A recognized thought leader in global accounting education, Sripal has authored content for Becker Professional Education and has spoken at prestigious forums including AICPA ENGAGE. He has also delivered sessions and collaborated with leading organizations including Microsoft, Deloitte, Wells Fargo, Reliance, AIG, and other multinational corporations.

He is also the Founder of AI Sripal, an AI-powered learning and career assistant designed to support students and professionals across global accounting and finance qualifications, including CPA, CMA, EA, CIA, ACCA, and CFA.

Beyond education, Sripal serves on the advisory boards of several globally recognized accounting and business process outsourcing organizations, including Analytix Solutions, QX Global Group, SandMartin, and Oremus Corporation, contributing insights on talent development, global accounting, technology, and professional education.

Through Simandhar Education, he has mentored thousands of students and professionals, helping them build successful global careers across accounting, finance, taxation, audit, advisory, and leadership roles.

Driven by the belief that education can transform lives, Sripal continues to advocate lifelong learning, global qualifications, leadership development, and future-ready skills for finance professionals in the age of AI.

www.ingramcontent.com/pod-product-compliance
Lightning Source LLC
LaVergne TN
LVHW090403210926
848480LV00002B/435
* 9 7 9 8 9 0 4 5 1 6 5 5 0 *